CON- 6 $/4 95

SHLEPPING THE EXILE

SHLEPPING THE EXILE

by

Michael Wex

Mosaic Press
Oakville-New York-London

Canadian Cataloguing in Publication Data

Wex, Michael, 1954-
Shlepping the Exile

ISBN   0-88962-542-5

I. Title.

PS8595.E955E94 1993   C813'.54   C93-093403-2
PR9199.3.W494E94 1993

Published by MOSAIC PRESS, P.O. Box 1032, Oakville, Ontario L6J
5E9, Canada.   Offices and warehouse at 1252 Speers Road, Units
#1&2, Oakville, Ontario, L6L 5N9, Canada.

Mosaic Press acknowledges the assistance of the Canada Council and
the Ontario Arts Council in support of its publishing programme.

The author would like to acknowledge the support and assistance of
the Toronto Arts Council in the completion of this book.

Design by Patty Gallinger
Typeset by Jackie Ernst

Printed and bound in Canada.

ISBN   0-88962-542-5   PB

MOSAIC PRESS:
In Canada:
    MOSAIC PRESS, 1252 Speers Road, Units 1&2, Oakville, Ontario
L6L 5N9, Canada. P.O. Box 1032, Oakville, Ontario L6J 5E9.
In the U.K.:
    John Calder (Publishers) Ltd., 9-15 Neal Street, London, WCZH
9TU, England

Dedication

In memory of my mother

A glossary of Yiddish and Hebrew terms will be
found at the end of the volume.

THE INFANCY NARRATIVE

Every candy store on earth smells of candy--it's self-evident. A fish store smells of fish, a fruit store of fruit, and a candy store smells *dekh* of candy.

Well, I got news for you, mister. My father, in addition to owning the only *shoymer shabbes* candy store between Winnipeg and the Rockies, had the further distinction of owning the only candy store in the world to--*what?* To sell Yiddish newspapers? To kick out the kids who bought the candy before they had a chance to buy it? --*What?* You've never been in a candy store? --No! The only candy store in the world to smell of gallnuts, the stuff they use to make the ink for Torahs, tefillin and mezuzas. After all, a man with his education, why shouldn't he round out his income a little, and be a bit of a big shot besides? So he became the town's scribe and cantor, and still had time to run a candy store ten hours a day.

The gallnuts were bad enough, but with his passion for righteousness it could go you dark in the eyes. I once tried to tell him that children recoil from being called the spawn of a hanged bastard, from being told that their parents are not their parents, but only enterprising goyim who bought them for one bottle of whisky and would soon be trading them for another. It was bad for business, I told him. "But I say it all in Jewish," he protested. It wasn't him, there was something wrong with the kids. "Everywhere in the world a child loves sweets, but in Canada they run from candy like from poison. Go know...I should become a coffin-maker, and, you'll pardon the expression, their Jesus would come and they'd all live forever, God protect us. Ach, I should have stayed in Shanghai."

I didn't have to tell him that Shanghai--which he'd somehow snuck into in 1941 and which has attained undying fame in Israel as my birthplace--his beloved Shanghai was now in the hands of the royte gelle, the red yellow men, and that his way of life was, to say the least, frowned upon by the authorities. Why bother? Even I knew that he wasn't talking about the present, but about the Shanghai where he waited for years to get out, and got screwed, like Jacob, in the end. Despite the Japanese, the war, and the renowned degeneracy of the place, Shanghai had had a small but very vital religious community, and when he spoke of Shanghai, my father did not mean the sin city of the east but the shtetl-within-a-ghetto in which he had lived. Economics aside, it was a Jewish paradise beside the shithole he was living in now.

"For you, my son," he'd say, patting me on my yarmulke, "For you I want something better than a candy store surrounded by cowboys. You, you've got an iron head on those skinny shoulders of yours, and after you're bar mitzvah we'll send you off to a great yeshiva in New York, and you'll grow up and become a great rabbi just like my father and my grandfather and his father before him. To think, Shaye Levkes, the ilu, the prodigy of the great yeshiva of Lomza, is owning a candy store at the end of the world. Master of the Universe, what is a man that you should pay him any attention? Don't bother to answer...A candy store, ekh mir a sustenance."

"But tatte, why didn't you take smikhe?" This had bothered me for years. He had all the knowledge of a rabbi and could have passed the standard examination while scooping gumballs out of a glass bowl. "You know enough, you could have been a rav anywhere. You can even speak English--real English, like a lawyer--when you want to."

He would tug at his beard, and a look would come into his eyes as if he had just been roused from the sweetest of slumbers. "You wouldn't understand." Then, breathlessly, as if he had spilled some great secret, he'd add, "It's forbidden to make money from Torah."

"And for me it's ok?"

"I'm still living in the old country; you're living here. In English there's a saying, 'You take the high road, I'll take the low road.'. You know what it means?"

"Are you kidding?"

"You're a smart boy, but you're still a boy, after all. It means that if you're going to end up in the cemetery, you might as well get there first class. Just don't go against the Torah. You understand?"

Yes, no, it made no difference. One way it wasn't explained, the other I got a klap in the head. So I understood everything. I was, after all, a Jew with beard and sidelocks. Uh, a Jew. With sidelocks. And hidden away in the midst of my father's cantorial records--Rosenblatt, Sirota, Leibele Waldman, he had em all--hidden away there, one, just one, unprepossessing little bombshell: Elvis Presley. And in my bedroom, between the mattress and the box-spring where my mother wouldn't find it--go know she'd lift up the mattress when making the bed--one copy, slick and nearly new, smelling of plastic and glossy paper; one copy--gotenyu, my hands still tremble just thinking about it--of *Nudist Life*. Shmiley Greenberg gave it to me after I found him whacking off on his tsitses. Elvis, nudists, I may have had payes, but *I* was hip. Who the hell wanted to be a rabbi and spend the rest of his life deciding which chickens were kosher and which had to be thrown away to the goyim? I knew what *I* wanted. I was gonna be the nudist Elvis Presley, performing only in nudist camps, singing *Heartbreak Hotel* to audiences full of girls, women, female babies who didn't care if I looked at their tits--Jesus Christ, they *wanted* me to look at their tits, not to mention their tukheses and you know whats--and who I didn't care if they looked at my mileh no matter how hard it was, and who'd all want to touch it and want me to touch them and feel their dewy wetness (I got the phrase from a book of Shmiley's). And finally...twelve times a day. A rabbi? Two weeks a month you can't even touch her, and even when you can she's always the same one. Unless...unless I could start a new kind of hasidism--me, Yoine Levkes, the davening Jewish nudist with his ballbearing hips, and daven and sing Yiddish folk songs to roomsful of girls, women...

"I think they get injections or something." Shmiley was in one of his speculative moods. We were sitting in the shell of a dead Hudson in the field at the corner of his street.

"Who?"

"Those guys in the nudist pictures."

I hadn't noticed the guys, but I wanted to look sophisticated. "What kind of injections?"

"You know, to keep them from getting boners."

"You mean just for the pictures?"

"No, asshole, all the time. Or else how could they walk around? When you get to be my age, you'll find out how embarrassing it is."

Shmiley was fifteen, just over two years older than me, but between my having skipped a grade and his having flunked one, we were in the same class, and as the only Jews, were forced to stick together. We weren't really friends. Shmiley was always talking about his real friends, whom I never saw (they went to another school or something), but he was the only person who was still growing that I talked to with any regularity, except to tell them to fuck off. When you're the only kid with payes in a town where they don't like Jews much to begin with, and are a suck in school besides, life can be a little difficult. Like they used to come from miles in every direction to stare at me, throw things and kick my ass. The guys I could handle all right. I couldn't really fight, but I was vicious, crazy enough that it wasn't worthwhile to do anything more than laugh and throw things. That I could take. It was the girls. To have some bright little blossom come up to me on Tenth Street, have her smile and "bump" gently into me--this was grade eight, remember--then look into my face, deep into my eyes and hiss, "I like your curls, Jewboy," that's what sent me home in tears. So when Shmiley had nothing better to do, he let me hang around with him, and I thanked God for the chance.

To kill the time when he wasn't around, I made friends with a mailbox. Down the street from the store, there was one of those old mailboxes, the kind they just hung up on a lamppost, and I used to stand there for hours at a time reading comics, waiting for people to come by and mail letters. When they did, as long as they were grown-ups, I'd put on my friendliest voice and wish them a good day. I enjoyed it. My friendliest voice consisted of a pleasant Irish lilt wrapped around a "Top o' the morning'. And how are you today?" uttered with alacrity no matter what the time. I'd heard it in some old movie with Pat O'Brien or Barry Fitzgerald and had been so struck by its irreproachable goyishness that I decided to use it in daily speech whenever I got the chance. You can imagine my delight on discovering that one of the old ladies who used the mailbox was named Mrs. Clancy. Three or four times a week I got to say "Top o' the mornin', Mrs. Clancy," and she'd answer me back and never ask about my beanie or those funny little curls.

Apart from the mailbox, there was no one but Shmiley. He was a bit of a dope, but you could talk to him, and I admired the way he'd overcome his immigrant background. Shmiley acted just like everybody else. His father ran the kheyder: his English was lousy, he had no trade, so they put him to work teaching children. The other kids told me I was lucky to study with my father; old man Greenberg was a sadist who used to knock them around just for the hell of it. Looking at Shmiley, I could believe it.

"Like just before school ended," he was saying, "I was sitting in geography and turned around to have a look at the clock, and whaddya think I saw? Rosalie Tompkins, you know how she used to sit behind me except in the next row, she's sitting there with her legs wide open, and guess what? She's wearing stockings. Real nylons. I could see the garters and her panties jammed right into her crack. Amazing. Anyway, I'm sitting there with this huge one on, and all of a sudden Kemp tells me to stand up and tell him about the fucking Canadian Shield. Jeesus, I knew it, but I was afraid to stand up, so I had to sit there like a dummy. The one time all year I know something, and my dick's standing out a yard long...I'll tell ya, the minute I got home, I locked myself in the bathroom, and all I could see was those garters and panties. Whew."

Rosalie Tompkins weighed about a hundred and sixty pounds, was covered in pimples, and was rumoured to do it with dogs for money, but I just sat and smiled and commiserated. If I didn't, he'd just say, "So how many hairs you got on *your* balls, eh, pisher?" and I didn't need to hear it again.

"How many broads you think I've felt up?" One of Shmiley's favourite questions.

"I don't know."

"More than you could count."

"Ah, come on. There aren't that many broads"--God, how I loved that word--"There aren't that many broads in the world."

"Well, more than you, anyway. And you know what I've discovered?" He assumed the tone of Dr. Ehrlich announcing the magic bullet. "You know what I've discovered? Shiksas wear black bras."

Just like that, no trace of emotion in his voice. This was science.

"Black bras?"

"Black bras. Like in the dirty pictures."

"All of them?"

"As far as I can figure out." That meant all of them.

"So they all look like dirty pictures?"

"You got it."

"Even the ugly ones?"

"Even the ugly ones."

"Even Miss Featherstone?" She was our English teacher. She was about ninety years old, and looked like a blue-haired ironing board.

"Even Miss Featherstone...Jesus, imagine that." For a second, he sounded almost wistful. "Miss Featherstone dressed up like Marilyn Monroe--and she wants you to do it to her! 'Stanley Greenberg,'" he said in a quavering falsetto, "'You'll stay after class tonight and lick out the insides of my black bra. And don't let me catch you misbehaving again.'" We laughed 'til we were almost sick, Shmiley, his hands perpendicular to his nipples, jumping up and down on the Hudson's sprung seat, gesturing to me with his head, screaming, "Fuck me, you fine little rabbi, fuck me!" until a real falsetto cut in. "Shmiley! Stanley! Kim-zhe shoyn ahaym. Se vert alles shoyn kalt." So Shmiley went home to dinner and I went off for my evening Talmud lesson in the little apartment in back of the store.

When I got there, I could hardly squeeze through the door. The place was packed with just about every immigrant Jew in town, all of them clustered around a short, unshaven figure who looked like one of the fly-specked lightbulbs in the window, and who was holding forth in a mixture of Yiddish, Polish, English and a little Japanese. Crowds weren't unusual in the store. Because of my father's position in the community, it served as a sort of clubhouse for the town's religious and immigrant Jews, who would often gather in the evening to pick up their copies of the *Foverts* and *Tog* and swap stories about each other. Sometimes they'd come later, alone, and my father would lock the door connecting to our apartment, imprisoning my mother and me in our three rooms and kitchen while he listened to the problem and offered his advice. I never managed to catch more than a few words, usually "a blondeh shiksa a karnoseh"--a blond, pug-nosed shiksa--from the women, and "milkman", always the milkman, from the men. Whatever they wanted, they all came, and except for the ones who came alone--*that* went only to my mother, and in Polish--we heard all about it afterwards, so that even as a child I had an intimate knowledge of the intimate lives of various men and women, men and women who looked to the outside world like nothing at all, nobodies, pipsqueaks, funny-looking Jews in cheap suits with patterns like car seats, skulking by at the edge of the street and talking loudly and with their hands in some ridiculous foreign gibberish. "Talk white, Ikey," the cowboys used to yell, and the farmers, Ukrainians all, would just smile in their drunkenness, once in a while greeting them with *"Bay zhidov"*, "Let's get the Jews". But I knew the privities of these shopkeepers and junkmen, and no greater company has ever faced the snares and temptations of a scurvy and murderous world. You can have your Achilles, your Horatius, your Alexander. Take them, and go in good health. Give me the beaten and bourgeois Jews, men who looked into the jaws of danger and turned the other cheek, they shouldn't have to see it. Their names alone tell their story; their names, terrible as an army with banners, solid as the ships of Homer:

Avrum Oyg, Abie Eye, for he had but one; Avrum Hoyker, Abie Hunchback--he had a bit of a stoop; Avrum Karlik, Abie Midget, stood five foot two; Avrum Vayb, Abie Wife, who started every sentence with "my wife says"; Avrum Doktor, Abie Doctor--he wore glasses; and Stam Avrum, Just Plain Abe--they hadn't found anything wrong with him, yet.

They were first cousins, the sons of six brothers from one village, and had all been named for their grandfather. The words "Abe Goldstein" could no longer signify, so they were named for their afflictions, and, thank God, they were all afflicted. Even Stam Avrum. He devoted his life to the acquisition of some sort of illness or disfigurement in order that he, too, might acquire a decent nickname. Abe Goldsteins-who needs them?

And there were others on the roll of honour: Berel Kucker, Di Eyer Meydelekh, Khave Lip, Khaim Mes, and Mendel Efsher. Berel the Shit, who used to beat his wife; the Egg Girls--their mother, Shifra Dropdead, sold eggs from door to door; Khave Lip, whose mouth was crooked as the result of a stroke; Khaim Corpse--Khaim means life--the head of the burial society; and Mendel Maybe, after his way of answering any question: S'regnt, Mendel? Efsher. But you're soaking wet. Efsher it burst only one cloud.

There were others, but these were the regulars. My father was particularly friendly with the Corpse and Maybe, who were both religious, and had I not been too young for some, too old for the others, I would have been stuck with their kids. Their Marvins and Sheldons and Marcias and Carolyns were known to adepts as the little hunchbacks, the little wives, the little shits, and, in the case of Mendel Efsher, Shmiley's father, di kleyne efsharusn, the small possibilities.

We, too, had been blessed. My father was known as Shaye Griner, Isaiah the Greenhorn, not because he was any more of a greenhorn than the rest of them, but because he had stayed religious and never even shaved off his beard. They used to sing him some dopey Yiddish song, from the thirties, I think:

> Yankel Doodle went to town
> Rayten af a ferdl,
> Er geyt arayn in barber shop
> Un shert op dos berdl.
> Yankel Doodle sher es op,
> Yankel Doodle dendy,
> Gey arum, zay nisht ken glomp,
> Un gib di vayber kendy.

Strangely enough, my mother was not called Rukhl Grineh or even Rukhl Shaye's. Instead, she was known as Rukhl Mayn Heyliker Tatte, Rachel-My-Sainted-Father, after her habit of referring to the customs and sayings of her father, the rabbi of some eastern Polish hellhole, in connection with just about anything you could mention. When she caught me trying to slick my hair into an Elvis cut with the help of a jar of chicken shmaltz, she took me aside and, never losing her temper for a moment, said to me, "Mayn heiliker tatte fleg zugn az dem, velkher leygt dem kop in shmaltz arayn, vakst shmaltz tsvishn di oyren." "He who sticks his head in fat grows fat between the ears." I couldn't understand her any better than I could my father. She often used to tell me that until she was married she never had any mind of her own.

I, of course, never had any mind at all--as if I had any choice in the matter--and they used to call me Yoine Payes. It may not have been terribly complimentary, being of a piece with Shaye Griner (the name, I mean), but I liked it all the same. No other kid had a nickname of his own, and if being called Payes was the price I had to pay to be part of the gang--and all I wanted was to be part of a gang, any gang--well, so be it. There's plenty worse things they could have called me. My closest friends were a juvenile delinquent, an inanimate object, and a group of men whose youngest member was my father.

Right now, though, the gang was too busy gaping at this new guy even to notice my presence. And as for me--despite the crowd, despite the visitor, it was my father who caught my eye as soon as I walked into the store. One of his eyes was narrowed right at me, fixing me in a beam of hatred like the death rays in the comics. The other was closed. He tugged significantly at the tip of his pointy beard, ran his tongue lightly over his lips. I looked up to heaven, the view was clouded by an old Coca Cola sign covering a hole in the ceiling, and begged the Lord to deliver me, if not for my own sake, then for the merits of my holy ancestors. Tatte's face told me that further prayers would be vain; I should thank God and His providence for the vast crowd which would keep him from beating me like a broom before they departed. By then he might have cooled down enough to wave me about his head three times--like a penitential chicken on the eve of Yom Kippur--and then just throw me away.

Mute, terrified, I stood pondering the whole list of my possible sins, when I was suddenly swept up from behind and raised aloft above the heads of the crowd. "Bring me my chariot of fire!" thought I. "Let me ascend with thy prophet and dwell in thy palace all the days of my life. These boast of soda-pop, those of the *Forverts*; but we boast the name of the Lord our God. They will collapse and fall, but we shall stand up and be established. Deliverance belongs to the Lord!"

Afire with piety rewarded, I was snapped out of reverie by a booming, somewhat nasal voice which shared my own tones of exultation. "And is this him?" it screamed in Yiddish. "This must be him. The baby. Look how big he's grown. Looks just like his father...Tell me, boy, do you remember me?" O God, let me die with the Philistines. "No?" He tossed me up and caught me with a grunt. "Well, come down here and shake hands like a human being." He set me down on the floor, back in the belly of the beast, hitched up his right sleeve, extended his hand to mine, bowed slightly and clicked his heels. "Yoine Levkes, I presume?" I sure as hell wasn't Dr. Livingstone. "Kalman Holzhacker, operating under the name Crispin Bismarck, at your service. A great pleasure. Now tell me about yourself, young man. Shoyr she-nugakh es ha-puroh, a bull which has gored a cow"--from the tractate *Bava Kamma*-- "What are you going to do? Wait, don't answer. Plenty of time for that later. Tell me of the progress of your soul on this rounded ball of terra firma." He said the last two words in Latin. "You a good boy? Making out?" This in English. I was sure he had taken me for Shmiley. "Well, now that we know all about you--oh, what beautiful long payes you have! Hey, Shaye, you want the kids should call him Curly? You're not in the old country anymore--now that we know all about you, it's time to tell you a thing or two about me." All I wanted was for him to let go of my hand. He clicked his heels and bowed again, finally letting my hand drop, and saluted. "As I said before, Kalman Holzhacker, doing business under the name Crispin Bismarck, *at your service, Monsieur*." He reached into his pocket, pulled out the biggest business card I'd ever seen and shoved it into my hand, commanding me to read it later. "No, you won't have time. Give it here." He grabbed it back, and announced to me in English, "I like my whisky straight, my women bent, and my folks was all Frenchmen."

Frenchmen, that's it! It's Kalman Franzoys, Kalman Frenchman, the hero of the Shanghai ghetto, and all my dreams come true. After my father's sainted grandfather, who had been an important figure in the final stages of classical hasidism, Kalman Franzoys was the subject of more of my parents' stories than any single human being--and not for reasons of piety. Kalman was a heretic, a nut, and a fine human being. One step ahead of the Nazis, he refused to leave Europe before he had rescued the Rebbe of Dlugaszow, a boyhood friend of his; yet he believed in nothing and mocked religious life and observance. He was a liar and a braggart. He blew his own horn so hard that he had gone deaf in one ear. His father had been one of the greatest Talmudists of his day, and had sent Kalman to the greatest yeshivas under the greatest rabbis. Kalman was always the star student, but the germ of decay was already there. He seemed to devour the material with his head, while his heart remained untouched. About such as him, who know and do not do, the gemore says it were better for them never to have been born.

It was said that he had once gone to the Chofetz Chaim, the He-Who-Desires-Life, the legendary scholar and saint Rabbi Yisroel Meyer Ha-Cohen of Radun, and attempted to prove to him the non-existence of God solely on the basis of the Talmud and its standard commentaries. It was further said that at the close of their discussion, the Chofetz Chaim burst into tears, some say because he had lost.

He was a poet, having published several volumes of Yiddish verse which had already become classics. He was a polyglot, speaking God knows how many languages, and all of them with the same Galician Yiddish accent. He had lived in Paris since before World War I. He knew Chagall and Leon Trotsky, the Lubavitcher Rebbe and John Cameron Swayze. He claimed that Frank Sinatra was Jewish and had been kidnapped by Italian-based gypsies who believed that his celestial crooning would bring on the advent of the Messiah. He claimed the Messiah was an invention of the Italians, a Judaized version of the cults surrounding the Roman emperors. He was a rhetor, a sinner and one who brought the multitude to sin. He was the best friend my father ever had, at least when they were in Shanghai, but God forbid he should have two such friends. Each, said my father, saw in the other what he could have become had he wanted to; each was drawn to the other by virtue of a fundamental agreement on one point of principle-- a Jew was a Jew, no matter what he thought he was. And Kalman, for all his heresy, was a distinctively *Jewish* heretic.

Kalman Franzoys. Whether I should believe all the stories- -my father kept mentioning "hidden depths" to the man--I didn't know, but that he'd delivered me for the time being from certain death--just as he did with the saintly Dlugaszower Rebbe--was enough to convince me of anything. My old man's anger was swift and implacable until two hours after the outburst, when he would give me a pinch in the cheek and send me out to play with my friends, and nothing had ever checked it before. He'd hit me in the shul or on the street, bawl me out--in Yiddish--in front of the whole school on parents' presentation day for slouching or mumbling. If Kalman Franzoys could stop him for even a few minutes, why couldn't he have stopped the Nazis and the Japanese?

"Shaye," he bellowed, turning away from me, "A fine boy, but he doesn't talk. Tell him that a Jew needs a tongue in this world." He began giggling, then added, "Your townspeople evince a true appreciation of genius. I must go now to dine. But mark my words, tomorrow shall be yours." He swept out of the store, knocking two or three people almost to the floor, and hurrying Khazkel Baalebos, the real-estate man and self-confessed big-shot, along in front of him.

The crowd was murmuring its excitement and admiration, the words "and a friend of Shaye Griner's yet," being added to every encomium of Kalman's bravery, poetic talent or worldwide fame, until my father, staring balefully at an almost empty soda cooler, finally began chanting the Confession traditionally recited on the way to certain death. They took the hint, but it was me at whom he was looking; and when he told me that in these times a boy should always have the respect to accompany his father's singing, I damn near went with them.

After he had locked the street door and hung out the "closed" sign, my father went over to the door at the back which led to our apartment, opened it, bowed, and asked me if the young man who seems to be such an authority on women--their composition, construction, and secret places--could spare a few moments from his rarefied speculation on khalals--empty cavities, sockets--to engage in civilized conversation with the wretches who had been cursed by God--for what sins he could not imagine--the unfortunate beings who had been chosen-- "Ha, chosen! The people of Israel were chosen, your mother and I were condemned while our souls were yet in the Garden of Eden"--the dust and ashes who had accomplished the miracle of uniting to produce a dungheap--just a few moments' discussion, if you please.

He slammed the door to and walked silently over to his chair. "Please sit down, Reb Noyef, Mr. Lecher." He motioned me to a chair as if I were a visitor unsure of where to sit, and waited for my mother to come in from the kitchen. "Rukhl, kim shoyn. Come on, already. Reb Noyef has to leave soon. Reb Noyef has an appointment in a nudist colony." He sneered the last two words in English. My mother came in already, walking as if her feet were bound and with her face the colour of cheesecloth. She went and stood by my father's chair.

"Shaye, take it easy. He's only a boy."

"Boy, shmoy. *This* wasn't enough." He threw something to the floor. "It wasn't enough to have those vultures descend on me and clean me out of a whole store soda-pop, I have to find on the same day that my son, my only child, my heir, the great grandson of the holy Garland of Gold, may his merits protect us, this my son is sneaking into my house, a house containing holy books, a house containing a scroll of the Torah itself"--a scroll he had been writing in his spare time for over two years now--"What? What has he been sneaking in? Tell me, Rukhl, what has he been sneaking in while his parents break their backs he shouldn't have to spend his life in a candy store doling out poison to vipers? Has he been sneaking in Spinoza? Spinoza I could face. Spinoza I could refute. Has he been sneaking in comic books? This kind of foolishness I permit him to read. 'He's only a boy,' Rukhl, he'd read them anyway. We also had foolishness in the old country. So not Spinoza, not comic books, not Karl Marx or Bergson. What, then, has he been sneaking in, you ask? A good question, my wife. What *has* he been sneaking in?" And he held up my copy of *Heartbreak Hotel*. They'd found everything, and everything was lost. "Elvis Shaygets Presley, the lascivious howler, the bum that not even a goy like Ed Solomon wants should be on his parade of television foolishness. And where did he sneak it? You would think that even Mr. Insolent Stiff Neck would have the decency to hide such garbage under his dirty laundry or with his library of fine art books." I winced again. "But no, not this one. Right here. Right here between Yossele Rosenblatt singing *Eli Eli* and

Jan Peerce's *A Din Toyre Mit Got*, here resides the son of Belial singing what is it?" He looked at the label. "*Heartbreak Hotel*.

"Now, my son. I want you should fartaytsh, explain, for me the meaning of this saying of your sage, Rabbi Elvis ben Orleh, Elvis the son of foreskin, 'heartbreak hotel'...What, you sit like a mute. All of a sudden Kalman Franzoys becomes a prophet? Nu, still no answer? Then I'll explain it for you. Heartbreak, in Jewish this is a tsebrokhn harts. And hotel? This is an akhsanye, a place where you stay for but a night. Now, what is another way of saying that somebody is with a tsebrokhn harts? Correct, that the event itself is hartsraysndik. And what means hartsraysndik? Something vus rayst oop by emetsen dos harts, something which rips his heart out. And where does this tearing out of the heart take place? Takeh in the akhsanye, the place where he stays for only one night. Nu, my ka mashmo lan? What does this teach us? A deep and profound moral lesson: that before I throw you out of this house for once and for all, I'm going first to rip your heart from your chest for killing your mother and me! Farshteyst? Heart, veins, arteries, the whole story straight from your chest and leave it for the dogs, like the blood of the wicked in the days of the prophets. Any questions thus far?"

I shook my head mutely and wished I were dead. "Good," he continued, "Mr. Wolf-In-Sheep's-Clothing understands everything. But don't leave yet, Mr. Whose-Mind-Is-Lower-Than-Mud. I have a further matter to discuss with you. But let us first bring this business to a close." He raised the record until it was level with his shoulders, holding it before his face like the magbieh who holds the Torah in the synagogue while it is being bound and wrapped. *Heartbreak Hotel*, the unread Torah of my youth; *Heartbreak Hotel*, which I had never had the chance to play, defiled by the hands of an unbeliever. Arise, O Lord, and let thine enemies be scattered.

He held it there briefly, read off the title once again, along with the writing credit, time, label and serial number, gently lowered the disc, holding it by the edges, until it was perpendicular to his chest, dropped one hand, and with the other flung it at me with all his might.

My father's athletic ability was that of the average Torah scribe and cantor, and the record would have glanced off the top of the chair, had my mother's sudden scream not startled me into jumping. The record bounced off my forehead and fell to the floor. My father sprang up, grabbed it, and began beating me over the head with it, finally throwing it back to the floor and stomping on it 'til it broke.

"Shaye, Shaye, Shaye!" My mother began to shriek--or had she started when he went to throw the record?--and asked if he had gone mad. He told her. He commanded her to keep silent. I was bent down on the floor, holding my head with one hand and gathering relics with the other. Between tears and terror, I could barely see; I reached out and took anything that came into my hand, hoping to save the label, just to show that once, if only once, I, too, had been a typical teenager, even if I was only twelve years old.

Meanwhile, my mother was telling my father that he should shut up, that the Angel of Silence should take him and all his forebears to all the black years, and somehow telling me at the same time to go into the kitchen, put a cold compress on my head, and she'd be in in a minute to look after me. I would live, she was sure; as for my father, I should kiss him goodbye if I liked the taste of snakeskin, and begin practising the Mourner's Kaddish.

I closed the kitchen door, lay the remains of my virgin record to rest on the counter and followed my mother's orders. Sitting there with a soaking fleysheke towel against my forehead, I was too upset to want to hear that was going on in the next room. I couldn't understand Polish anyway, so I began to sort through the pieces of the record to see if I could glue it back together somehow. I'd only managed to pick up about half of it, and what I had thought was the label turned out to be the piece of paper my father had flung to the floor at the beginning of our discussion. I picked it up and squinted at it. It was a printed invitation, in Yiddish:

Khokkem Ba Le-Ir
A Sage Cometh to Town
It is with the greatest of pleasure that we extend you our most cordial invitation to join with us in a gala reception for the world-renowned scholar and poet, an ordained graduate of the Yeshiva of Mir, the hero of the Exile of Shanghai,

KALMAN HOLZHACKER
(known to his intimates as Franzoys),
to be held at five o'clock this afternoon in the vast meeting
hall,

SAM'S CANDY AND SMOKES,
3512 19th St.
Your presence is earnestly besought.
The K. Holzhacker (Franzoys) Reception Committee

The name and address of my father's vast meeting hall had
been pencilled in in red, as had an addendum at the bottom
marked N.B., to the effect that no contributions would be
solicited.

I scratched my head, wincing again with the pain, and
watched the lightbulb come on above me: Kalman had invited
them himself. And with the light there came understanding.
"Shaye, do you think you can speak with the boy like a human
being?" They were back to Yiddish; fate was really impending.
"My holy father always used to say that no scholar on earth has
the power to see through the veil of a boy's mind, and that a
boy's sins of curiosity should be taken lightly--the same curiosity
will one day be applied to Torah. So don't be too hard on the
boy."

"The boy"--Jewish parents always discuss their children as
if they were a thing apart. Substitute the car, the floor. "Shaye,
leave the floor alone. What harm can it do the car, one lousy
record?"

"What harm can it do the boy, one lousy record?"

"And this...this shmutz, this with the naketeh vayber?"

"Shaye, he not yet bar mitzvah even."

"Not yet bar mitzvah. An excuse. Not yet bar mitzvah and
already a sex pervert. Can this be bar mitzvah? Can this, with
its head, the inside of its head, between the legs of some fat
shiksa, approach the holy Torah? I ask you. For such sins, the
Lord annihilated the generation of the flood. 'The thoughts of
man's heart are evil from his youth,' He said. Before today I
never understood this verse. I had never seen an evil youth.
Playful, mischievous, but evil? Never. And in this one matter
my sins have warranted that my own son should be my rebbe.

Maybe the apikorism, the heretics, are right. Maybe the world
has no order. Ach, I don't know anymore."

He sounded a little calmer than before. Instead of raging,
he bristled.

"Your words should be as if they were never spoken. Is the
boy evil? Rebellious? Does he refuse to daven? Does he hate
to learn? Or try to cut off his payes? Come to your senses,
Shaye. I'm not saying that what he did is right. Never in my
life have I seen such a book. But think, Shaye, if they would
have had such books in Poland, would they not have circulated
in the yeshivas? Don't lie to me, my father was a rabbi,
remember. And if they would have been in the yeshivas in
communities of holiness and purity, by how much the more
should they be in the treyfene cities of the cowboys? It's a minor
sin. Take the book away from him--you've already done for the
record--and leave him be. Look at the date on this magazine.
It's six months old. In six months has he grown a foreskin?"

"Not for want of trying."

"Ah, there's no talking to you. Remember, Shaye, only a
fool has a beautiful world." I heard my mother get up.

"And I started making him tefillin already," my father
muttered as she came through the door.

After being meticulously examined and assuring her that it
was only a flesh wound, I entered the second of hell's seven
levels. "Yoinele, your father spoke in haste. You know what
he's like, especially where you're concerned. You've got to try
and understand what it's like for him, and for me, too. An
entire family killed during the War." So what else is new,
mama? Whenever I'm in trouble, it's the same story. "Brothers,
sisters, parents...and your father--he was already a widower
when the war broke out. Imagine, twenty-five years old,
married to a sickly and barren woman--I don't speak against
her, this is what she was--because of a promise made by your
grandfather at his bris, and one day, poof, she's no more. And
then Hitler and his hangmen...He wants you should be not
only a child but a sort of substitute for all these people. He
wants you should be, vi zugt men af english, larger than life,
you know what I mean. Not just a son, but...I don't know how
to explain to a child, you know Superman in the comical books?

Well, the way your father wants you should be is the way Superman is compared to other men. You understand now? You understand it would be hard enough for him and for you even if we were still in the old country, even if we were in America in a Jewish city like New York. But here, in the middle of nowhere, where the Jews are as vulgar as the goyim--Avrum Hoyker and Avrum Vayb and Khazkel Baalebos and all the rest of them aren't good enough even to lick your father's boots. And that pig Mendel. S'a melamed. *This* is the teacher. In the old country he wouldn't be fit to look after the bathhouse. A pig in his own dirt...A drinker, a philanderer, an I don't know what...And that boy of his, you watch, he'll yet be an Al Capone. Don't think I don't know where you came by that garbage, what's it called, *Nudist Life.* Your Shmiley has a big mouth, and I heard him telling other boys one day on Tenth Street how he goes up by the Ukrainians on the north side and buys them in their stores, they don't care who buys this shmutz so long as they get their money. I know all about your Shmiley, but I didn't say anything. Your father isn't so good at judging people--look at his friend from Shanghai, the hero--and I don't want to blacken Mendel Efsher in his eyes. Everybody but you he can forgive their sins. And besides, I know how hard it must be for you with the yarmulke and payes, I want you should at least have somebody your own age to talk to."

"Somebody my own age? Shmiley's my only friend. The other kids hate me."

"People are always afraid of anything that's different. That's why they've picked on us for so long. We stand out..Tell me, Shmiley's a smart boy?"

"Shmiley's a dope."

"You're in love with him? You'd follow him anywhere? You'd choose him for a friend?"

"Not if I had any choice. He only bothers with me when he's got nothing else to do."

"Good. Then maybe our Shmiley won't influence you too much more. But do try not to see so much of him."

"But nobody even talks to me, except to throw curses. Jewboy, they call me. And Curly. Kalman Franzoys was right. They run up to me and grab my payes and start going whoo-whoo-whoo-whoo like Curly in the Three Stooges. Whoo-

whoo-whoo-whoo, hey Moe, getta loada dis, a Jewboy. And then sometimes they take my yarmulke and start throwing it around and put it on and go meh, meh, meh, get outta da store, bom, doing imitations of tatte, and then they say fucking Jew."

"And that you killed their Jesus?"

"What?" I'd never heard this one before.

"No, no. Forget about it."

By this time I could barely speak for crying. I'd never really talked about my life before, except to say that school was fine or that I was on my way to the library and my family were doing just fine, and the sudden realization of just how miserable I really was, how much I hated everything and everyone around me, Jews, goyim, mailboxes, lampposts, the whole fucking town and everything in it, the novels and comics and gemore and occasional movies that served as my friends, the whole thing burst over me like a sudden storm--the ones the radio tells you are coming every day for days on end, and when they finally do show up everyone's already forgotten they're supposed to come and they've left all the windows open at home and set out for a picnic lunch in the Godforsaken plains or rolling foothills or grand coulees or whatever the hell kind of bullshit the wonderful God's country of Alberta is supposed to contain, and everybody gets soaked and catches pneumonia--double pneumonia--and dies.

"I hate this fucking place!" I wailed in English. "I wish I'd been born in Europe and then I could have died in a camp with everybody else. I wish it, I really do."

"Oy, Yoine, Yoinele mayns." Now she was crying, too. "Ret nisht azoy, don't talk like that. What can I do? What can I do for you? We can't go away from here. I don't like it any better than you do, but your father, he should live and be well, your father has his business here, such as it is, and we have to make the best of it. Remember, in an ort vus in im zenen ken mentshn nishtu, in a place where nobody is a mentsh, proobir di a mentsh tsu zayn, you should try to be one. Would you like better to go stay by your cousins in New York? We're not trying to get rid of you, we just want for you a little happiness."

"New York? I managed to blubber. "It's just as bad as here. When I was there in the summer a couple of years ago, the kids all made fun of me."

"What? For being Jewish? For wearing payes? In Williamsburg, Brooklyn?" My mother was incredulous.

"No, for being a goy," I screamed. "That's what they used to call me. Der goy, der shaygets, der cowboy. Hey cowboy, vus makhn di ferd, how are your horses? Jewboy, cowboy, if I'm going to be miserable, I'd rather be miserable with you." I threw my arms around her and for the last time in my life broke down crying on my mother's breast.

She rocked me and patted my head. I remembered how nice it was to be three: I may have been scared of everything under the sun, but I could always count on being taken care of.

"Your day will come. The day will come when you will laugh at all of them. Believe me."

Somehow I couldn't. Not only because I assumed that it's what every mother tells an unpopular twelve year old, but also because, as my tears abated, it occurred to me, for no reason at all, that Shmiley's mother probably told him exactly the same kind of stuff when he brought home a report card full of D's. The thought that Shmiley's mother, who was big and fat and the worst cook in the world, could consider somebody like Shmiley, not to mention the Shmiley himself, to be somehow above and beyond the rest of humanity deprived me of any sense of comfort. If people were really that stupid, then maybe the day would never come, maybe I'd have to spend the rest of my life apologizing to Serel Efsherke for not being as wonderful and dumb as her Shmiley. I could see no way out unless they were all killed.

"These things, these names they call you, why didn't you tell us?"

"What good would that do? You'd let me cut off my payes?"

"And do you want to?"

"Yes! Yes! Yes! I wanna look like everybody else. I wanna be like everybody else. I wanna go out with girls like everybody else."

"Girls, nokh." She sounded like she felt sorry for me. "Twelve years old, you're so interested in girls already."

"I'm almost bar mitzvah."

She chuckled. "And we stop you from seeing girls? Especially now, in the summer, does anybody tell you where to go, what to do?"

"And when could I go anywhere? Friday night it's shabbes, Saturday's not oys shabbes until way after nine. During the week I gotta be home to daven. When could I go? And even if I could, , who'd go with me the way I look? I told you, they laugh at me."

"All of them?"

"All of them. Why do you think I got that book?" I asked, seized by a sudden inspiration. "I've gotta find out about this stuff somewhere, or else--or else...you want me to grow up to be a pimp just so I can find out what it's all about? That's why guys become pimps, you know, so they can learn what they never had a chance to find out."

My mother was staring at me as if she'd gone into the Louvre and found Milton Berle where the Mona Lisa should be. "Bist metiref gevorn in gantsn, you gone completely crazy? I can't understand a word you're saying. What's all this about the pumps?"

In the heat of my eloquence, in the middle of all that Yiddish, I called a pimp a pimp, forgetting that to my mother a pimp was a thing that water came out of on farms. "It's English, Ma. A pimp"--I didn't know how to say it in Jewish, so I explained what I thought a pimp was. She got the general idea, and explained to me, since I was such a man of the world, exactly why pimps became pimps.

My disappointment was all the answer she needed. She gave me what to eat. "Nu, pimpele, nu, my little pump, forget all this foolishness and go to bed. I'll talk things over with your father.

*   *   *

If only destiny would have listened as well as my father. He, I mean my father, grabbed me the next morning as I was trying to sneak out through the store, coming up from behind and clapping a hand on my shoulder. The long arm of the gemore? Couldn't be; he didn't pinch me.

"Wait a minute, pardner." He grinned at his English. "I want you to know that what you did was wrong. Maybe I was too harsh, but you were still wrong, and I don't want you to do it again. As for the rest that your mother told me, I don't know what to say. I can't change these people. You've got to be strong. Look at yourself. Do you really think that throwing away your yarmulke and cutting off your payes, God forbid, would make you any more like them? You're too smart, too delicate in your soul, and thank God you've still got dus pintele yid, that point of Jewishness, burning inside you. And I can tell what kind of boy you are. No matter where you are or what you might be, it will never leave you. You couldn't be a goy if you wanted to." He was beaming with pride. My mother must have told him she'd take me and run away if he didn't apologize. He'd never done it before, not to me or to anybody else. Maybe the Messiah *was* coming. "Maybe it's true that in this kind of wilderness a man has to make compromises, but that kind of garbage no parent, not even the Ukrainians, would allow. Now, go along, buy yourself a present," he said, pressing a fifty-cent piece into my hand. "You'll learn today an hour early. We have a guest for dinner."

"A guest?" We never had guests in the house. They all stayed in the store.

"Kalman Franzoys."

"You'll let him in here? I thought you hated him." Thank God, everything was back to normal.

"Hate him? Why should I hate him?"

"The way you threw the invitation."

"The invitation I hate. Inviting the whole town to drink my soda-pop without even asking my permission I hate. But this doesn't mean that he isn't a fine man. With little things he goes too far, but I know, I have seen with my own eyes, that he is ready twenty-four hours a day to die for the sake of the Jewish people."

"And he's really a musmakh, he really has ordination?"

"He might not look it, but he is. Kalman is a man who pretends not to believe. But he does, and he is afraid of this belief. You wouldn't understand." Lately I wouldn't understand a lot. Maybe they thought I was dumb. Maybe I was. "He was given his smikhe when he was fourteen years old, this was still before World War I, but he told me that even then he was reading forbidden books. He says he doesn't believe, but in Shanghai I saw him expound Talmud hundreds of times, in such a way that only a man who studies regularly can. Watch him closely. You will see what happens to a Jew who denies himself what his soul thirsts for. Now, go, have a good time."

What did his soul thirst for? Did this mean I could look at all the *Nudist Lifes* I wanted to? Maybe I had to, or I would end up like Kalman. "But tatte, it's my duty to the pintele yid. I need to look at this stuff. I need to listen to Elvis. My soul thirsts for it--like a hart by flowing streams." My soul thirsted for anything that was female and naked, female and "scantily clad". Bathing suits, garter belts, vay iz mir. For months I could hardly think of anything besides my thoughts and their evil consequences. The Lord God of Israel made no move that did not depend directly upon my private thoughts and behaviour, and that damned *Nudist Life* could give us all an earthquake. Prudently, then, I took the money down to Squeaky's Used Book Exchange on Centre Street and bought a big hardcover book with pictures, about twenty years old and published in Moscow, all about the daily lives of Soviet minorities.

I was just about finished it when my mother knocked on my door and told me that my father was ready for our lesson. Though I would never have admitted it publicly, I loved studying gemore, even if I didn't want to be a rabbi. It was interesting, fun, and I was good at it. Studying alone with my father kept me too scared to fall behind, and I found when I was in New York that I was considerably more advanced than kids my age in yeshivas. My father threw in the occasional sermon, today's concerned filial piety, during which I usually tried to formulate unanswerable questions or resolve insoluble contradictions in the text, and the time usually went much more quickly than I wanted it to.

We were just about to progress to a new issue when a commotion was heard in the store, the voice of Kalman Franzoys announcing his arrival and adding that he hoped to see a little more of the boy then he had a chance to yesterday. My father looked at his watch in alarm, told me to hurry up and get dressed, and went out to the store to receive his guest.

We didn't have a dining room, so I planted myself at the kitchen table. I wore a blue jacket and a red bow tie. My hands were folded on the table and I had a self-consciously boyish grin on my face. Except for the payes, it could have been Thanksgiving. My mother, who was frantically worrying a chicken, told me to get out and go into the living room.

Kalman and my father were sitting across from each other with glasses of whisky in their hands. Kalman, as I'd already come to expect, was in the middle of saying something.

"And so you see, Reb Shaye, neither chance nor mere coincidence has brought me hither, off the beaten track though it be." He talked like a reform rabbi who's learned his Yiddish from the newspapers. "You and you alone have received the signal honour of being the first stop on my expedition. It is now ten years since we all left Shanghai, and on the occasion of this anniversary I have decided to visit as many of our former comrades as I can find, not for any particular purpose, mind you, simply that we might have the pleasure of seeing one another again and recalling the perils from which we have been delivered. From here I go to Winnipeg, thence to Montreal, and from there to the good old USA...Nu, tell me, Shaye, you're doing well with this candy store?" My father gave him the usual "Blessed be the Lord", fidgeting a bit with his whisky glass. Things could naturally be better, but so far he wasn't complaining. He wasn't *losing* money; from the mezuzas etcetera, he was doing ok, and the boy, thank God, he jerked his head in my direction, was, as Kalman could see for himself, growing into a prime specimen of Jewish manhood. "You said a mouthful," Kalman exclaimed in English, unaware that twenty-four hours earlier I had been a dangerous sex pervert. "Tony Curtis with payes. Nu, yingele," he continued, switching back to Yiddish, "Let's see how much you know." I sat back in my chair, preening myself. It was time for the gemore quiz. The usual simple questions, most of them on the tractate *Bava Metsiye*, which I had long ago mastered. I had trouble keeping the sneer off my face: I could see him turning to my father in fifteen minutes' time, sweat dripping from his upper lip at the prospect of being trounced by a twelve year old--I was no respecter of reputations--and reverently sighing, "Once in a century, Shaye. Once in a century."

I had him and I knew it, so I must have done a genuine double-take when I thought I heard him ask me if I spoke English. I begged his pardon, and he repeated the same question. Jerk. "Of course I speak English." This guy was a genius? He was probably going to ask me how you call a tablecloth.

"Of course 'of course'," he observed sardonically. "You were born in Canada?"

"No, sir." My "of course" may have been a little abrupt.

"And they speak English in Shanghai?"

"No, sir. Chinese." As if he didn't know.

"Oh, Chinese. So I assume then that you also speak Chinese." He sounded like a teacher trying to trick you into a confession.

"No," I answered, getting a little impatient. "When we left there I was still a baby."

"Oh. You see why I ask. In the natural course of events I could expect you to speak Chinese but not English. But you seem to be an unnatural little boy. Have I ever heard you speaking English? Yet I am fully cognizant of the fact that you are a native of Shanghai. You will please forgive me. Since you speak English so well, let us speak English together for a while. Agreed?" Fine by me. "Ho-kay, since you speak so good English, I would like you should tell me what it means the word divagate."

"Navigate?"

"No. Not navigate-to-steer-one's-course, divagate. You know? No? To divagate is zikh arumtsuvulgern. At least about your Jewish I don't have to ask. All right, let's see how much more English you know. Tell me, please, what it means the word tergiversate." Ter what? Whatever this game was, I didn't want to play anymore. I told him there was no such word in English, and with all due respect, I didn't like to be made fun of, especially in my own home. "Who's making fun?" His innocence sounded outraged. "I just want to see how smart you really are. Tergiversate," he stood up, pulled a pocket dictionary from inside his jacket, opened it with a flourish and thumbed through it as he returned to his seat. "Tergiversate, ah ha! 'To desert a cause or party; to become a renegade; to apostatize," with the accent on the last syllable. "Zikh shmadn, that is. You see. You say you speak English, but even as much as me you don't know. Nu, we'll give you one more chance. Now tell me, and I want you should think real hard, what is the meaning of the following-word-epigone?"

He wasn't going to get me again. I'd never heard the word in my life, but with my dreams of triumph shot to hell, I wasn't

going to let him take me three for three. I thought hard, looking
from Kalman to my father, anticipating laughter and disgust. I
thought harder, pulling the skin over my brow with such
intensity that soon I couldn't see anything but this stupid word,
I didn't even know how you spelled it, dancing in my head.

"Nu, yingele. The beggar is already by the third village."
I never realized how dumb that sounded in English.

"Ok. An epigone," I said, stalling for time, "An epigone,"
stretching it out syllable by syllable, "An epigone," and a quick
rush of breath, "An epigone is a klayn shvartserel vus voynt in
afrikeh, a little negro who lives in Africa."

"Wrong," he chortled. "Absolutely, positively, one hundred
and twenty percent--Wrong! A rakhmones on you, Shaye, your
boy is so dumb." He turned back to me. My father was wilting
with shame. I could already hear him: all day long he reads
books, but in *Nudist Life* the words aren't so important. Thanks
a lot, Mister Whoever-you-are; just when I was off the hook.
"An epigone," he was saying, "Is a follower what he's not so
good as the real thing. Like from your father, you, Yoine
Levkes, are an epigone. You understand?"

I understood, all right. He was my father's stooge, and it
was all a plot not to have to give in to my mother. Didn't have
the guts to finish me off himself. And that fake friendliness
over the gemore this afternoon--a trick to put me off my guard.
The hell with him! From this day forth we were sworn enemies,
fifty cents or no fifty cents. Him and his insidious friend. If he
likes to talk English so much, let him talk real English, like
"Fuck you, Charlie." English. A mageyfeh in English, the
plague take it.

"So, my semi-literate youthful friend," Kalman had switched
back to Jewish, "Your English is not so good as maybe you
thought. You know what the prophet Elijah said? He said, 'O
God, take away my life for I am not better than my fathers.' You
think you want to die? No? Good. We'll give you a chance to
stay alive..." I didn't want any favours. I wanted to die
tomorrow, after I'd bought every nudist magazine in the history
of the world and thrown them right in his face, and my father's,
too, screaming "These are your gods, O Israel!" as loud as I
could. I couldn't stand the idea of having my vocabulary
attacked. My one shred of self-respect pulled out from under

me the way a comic magician pulls a tablecloth from a fully-loaded table--the tablecloth comes out all right, but all the dishes fall to the floor.

My thoughts had no effect on Kalman's monologue, which just kept falling like rain. "Your father tells me..." He went on to mention the tractate we were studying, offering a brief summary of its contents and major problems. "This tractate I learned with your father in Shanghai. Since you're not so good in English, let's see how you come out in gemore." And he proceeded to examine me in minute detail on precisely those sections of the tractate which had eluded even the greatest commentators. I struggled through my explanations as best I could, tried to counter his counter-arguments, all the while wishing I had a stiletto to plunge into his breast. We went on like this for about half an hour--this guy knew his gemore, all right---when Kalman threw his hands into the air and cried out, "Enough! It looks like you'll live." He turned to my father and began to speak as if I were Rabbi Akiva revived. "Brilliant, marvelous, a real Jewish head." He had only tripped me up on the English, he said, because he expected any son of Shaye Levkes, not to mention the only one, to display such virtuosity in Talmud, and he wished to prevent my head from getting swollen. And also, he giggled, to add a little salt to the Talmudic discussion. He would have been suspicious had I known those words. He roared with laughter. I looked from him to my father again, not knowing what to think this time. My triumph made me feel even dumber, but I couldn't tell them why I looked so sheepish. This guy was too strange to make out.

My exhibition led them on to a barrage of reminiscences of their own yeshiva days. I excused myself and went to help my mother. She would have shooed me back, the kitchen was no place for a boy almost bar mitzvah, but dinner was already served.

It was one long memory. Afterwards, we retired to the living room, and Kalman began to speak of his life in Los Angeles. "The business is flourishing, thank God. I am now publishing more books and in bigger numbers than any Yiddish publisher in America."

"And you make a living from it?" asked my mother. "Does it even pay for itself? Yiddish publishing is not exactly the best-seller business. How many copies of a book can you sell?"

"Of poetry maybe a thousand, twice or three times that for the novels. No, you're absolutely right. The publishing, the Yiddish publishing, does not pay for itself."

"So how, then, are you flourishing so well?" my father asked.

"I have another business. It supports not only the publishing but also me, and very handsomely, if I say so myself."

"Another business?" my mother asked. "Nu, tell us what it is already," my father threw in.

"I don't know that all this business talk interests the boy." For once he was dead on.

"Boy, shmoy. It would do him good to hear how a man sacrifices himself for yiddishkayt. Go ahead, Kalman."

He stared down at the floor abashedly, blushing a little and shuffling his feet. I'd never have figured him for a blusher. I followed his eyes downward and noticed that his expensive-looking shoes were badly scuffed, the laces frayed. He coughed gently, cleared his throat, and, straightening up, began his story.

"Let me begin with a little history," he said. "When my late wife and I came to Los Angeles eight years ago, I was publishing Yiddish literature and going broke faster that I could starve." My parents looked at each other, nodding their heads in judicious sympathy. Only a madman would go into Yiddish publishing--most of the people who could still read it were too religious to want it. Kalman tugged at his suspenders and belched softly.

"Well, shortly after my arrival, I discovered, accidentally, and how it happened is no business of yours, that I had what you call in English a gift for the horses. You know what this means?" My parents did not, so Kalman had me explain. "I can see what you're thinking, that I support the Holzhacker Farlag from horse-racing bets. Wrong. The horse-racing is only the beginning." His whole tone had changed. It was still Kalman, but almost normal.

"As you know, a lot of people who are not so morally ay-ay-ay hang about the race tracks..." and Kalman, who had never been shy, had somehow managed to befriend one of them. A Jewish sharpie in the Mickey Cohen mold, by the name of Dutchy. Anyway, this Dutchy, who knew about Kalman's publishing, came to him one day with a proposition. As the result of an unexpected death, the local boys had nobody to run their magazine publishing business. Dutchy had told these boys about Kalman and his experience in the publishing field, and they were interested in talking to him.

He went to see them, they checked his background and police record, consulted with his bookie. A week later they asked would he like the job. Since they already owned the business, never mind whose name was on the registration, they were willing to hire him for a thirty-percent share of the profits, more money--he realized after seeing the books--than he had ever dreamed of.

"Would I like it?" Kalman asked. "Like Eisenhower should like a toupee...From nowhere I became editor and publisher of six, seven magazines, chiefly devoted to pictures of such things that let alone the boy, I know even you have never heard of."

The whole story had taken about an hour, and was full of mobsters, crooked cops, hijacked trucks, and everything else I'd ever seen in any gangster movie. And except for the cops, they were all Jewish. I thought it was great. My parents both looked as if they had just seen the Angel of Death. Their eyes were wide, their mouths open, their hands white on the arms of their chairs. They were still too numb to be angry.

"Yoine," croaked my mother, "I think you should go to your room."

She had to be kidding. I went off through the kitchen, taking care to close the door tight behind me, took my shoes off, slammed the door to my room, and tiptoed back through the dark kitchen, standing with my ear pressed to the door. I wasn't going to miss a single word.

"So." My father's voice had taken on the tone of a prosecuting attorney. "You began publishing these magazines in order to support your Yiddish literature?"

"Correct," said Kalman, "And I'm now publishing close to three million copies of different magazines every month. There are two series. One you can find on any newsstand, the others come wrapped in plastic and cost a small fortune--and they're the cheapest ones to make," he chuckled. He really seemed to enjoy putting one over on people. "You know, Shaye, they sell very well. I could arrange for..."

"In a store where I write tefillin? Doctors should make a living from you."

"All right, all right. I thought you might want to help further the cause of Yiddish literature."

"What *cause*? The cause of the Jewish goyim? For years I've defended you, Kalman. Underneath your, uh, unconventional exterior, I always said, there beat the heart of a saint. In such times as ours, I said, not all the saints will be rabbis--*I* the wonder of the Lomza yeshiva, said this--they will be saints for a corrupted people, saints who can reach those who have forgotten the Torah and its commandments. But I was stupid, too stupid to be a man, Kalman. You are a disgrace to our sufferings. Because of such as you, we've had already one Hitler. And now you want to bring on a second.'"

"Hitler, Shitler. I do what I do for the sake of the Jews. How can anyone believe such twelfth-century quatsch? I do it all for the Jews, and if I had my life to live over again, I'd do it all again. What the hell have you ever done for the Jews? With all your studying and praying and mumbling and making of incantations and amulets, what have you ever done for the Jews? Did you organize them in Shanghai? Did you save the Rebbe of Dlugaszow from the Nazis? Did you save anyone, anything, except your own stinking hide? Hitler, he throws at me. If there had been more like me, there wouldn't have been any Hitler. We would have stopped him before he could start, and if he would have started we would have used their own methods against them and at least got away with our lives. A rakhmones on you, Shaye. You think Hitler was a punishment from God? Hitler was a punishment from Hitler. You talk like he was supernatural; you, the big Jew, talk about Hitler like he was something besides bosser va-dom, flesh and blood. When you see a Hitler, you don't keep standing shminesre. You treat him before he treats you. And that's exactly what I'm doing. I'm feeding the goyim the same poison they want to give us. You know how much intermarriage goes on? We have to keep them in the slime where they belong. So I wrap up the poison like candy and give it to them, and use their money--believe me, you think you know these people, you don't know from nothing, I get fathers coming to see me with pictures of their daughters shtupping horses, and this is at least eighty percent of the population--and I use their money to exalt, to try to keep alive the only culture in the world that knows from good and evil, from life and death, and from life that's worse than death. But you have to open your eyes, Shaye. It's war, and we must fight like Joshua, not die like martyrs."

"But Joshua spoke with the spirit of the Lord."

"And I don't?"

"Kalman, you're mad. You're crazier than the Irgun-niks, as crazy, you should pardon the expression, as the Nazis themselves."

It had to happen. They always got on to Hitler. No matter where they started or what they did, there was always Hitler, waiting in the wings for the finale.

"We'll see who's crazy, Shaye. You wanted the boy should hear how a man sacrifices himself for yiddishkayt. Well, he heard. Not what you thought he would hear, but what you wanted him to hear. And it's not my fault you don't like it. For the sake of the Jews, I have thrown myself into the gutter, into the husks of the husks. For the sake of the Jews, I change my name to Crispin Bismarck--Bismarck, that pig--and as president and chairman, on paper, of Bismarck Publications, Los Angeles, California, USA, devote myself to turning out garbage so the Jewish nation can live again. So I can be Kalman Holzhacker, Kalman Franzoys who lived fifteen years in Paris writing poems in praise of God and His people, I spend my days as Crispin Bismarck, bringing out magazines called *Suave, Gallant, Nudist Life*--"

"What?!" my parents exclaimed in unison.

"*Suave, Gallant, Nudist Life*. I even write the last one. 'Naked as nature intended, we have returned to the state of nature from which...'"

"Enough already!" My father was shrieking. I heard his hand slam down, and a crash of breaking glass.

"Shaye! O my God, Shaye, you're bleeding all over the room." He must have put his fist right through the ashtray.

"Get out," my mother screamed, "Get out and don't come back. From today on, we don't know you, we never knew you, and we never want to know you."

I scurried back to my room on the verge of hysteria. I could hear my parents fulminating in the kitchen-- "And in front of the boy, yet." I was so agitated I couldn't think. Some of Kalman I liked, once I figured out the kind of tricks he liked to play, but the rest of him was even crazier than my parents. This guy thought he was meshiekh. He really believed that his dirty pictures were going to keep the Jews pure and save them from the ovens. I mean, they were a lot of fun to look at, but I couldn't see them doing anything but making guys hot. And the way he went on, me and Shmiley must be goyim just for looking. I didn't think I'd ever be able to look at a naked woman again. All I'd see was Kalman.

The next morning I found my father bent over his writing desk behind the counter. Despite the bandage on his hand, the gallnuts were in full bloom, but he was drawing crazy signs and pictures on the parchment, covering it with words that didn't exist. "This is a kmeye," he explained, "An amulet to ward off evil spirits and unwanted guests...What I told you before about Kalman, forget it. That man is possessed by an evil spirit. Forget him and his stories and his magazines. Never mention his name again. You understand?" I gave him my solemn word. "It were better that he'd never been born... Oh, before you go. Shmiley came by and said for you to go over to his house. Say hello to his parents for me."

Shmiley's house meant the vacant lot, and when I got there I found him in a state of exaltation. "You hear the news?" he asked me. "There's a new Jewish family just moved into town, over on the north side--they don't know no better--and, and they've got two daughters, yidishe tekhter," he added, making outlines of female figures in the air. "They're from Calgary. My mother knows them somehow. And these daughters, holy shit! One's fourteen and the other's twelve. The older one, that's mine, her tits are out to here and she wiggles like a slinky. And yours, she's not so built, but she's real cute, little and dark, and you know what? She said she likes to read. Just like you!" I was going to faint any second. "Anyway, they said that if we're not doing anything much today we should come over and get acquainted. And from the way they were looking, they meant *get acquainted.*"

"A-nu?" I asked in my old man voice. We looked at each other, burst out laughing, and hit the trail for the north side, my hand holding onto my yarmulke and my payes flapping in the wind.

The Good News

I

If only my father had had the courage to throw back his leonine, Talmudic head in what the goyim, the *ethical* goyim, would call a frenzy of legalistic rage, point his forefinger out the door, and say unto me with the ossified implacability of all the ages, "Avek fun mein tir, depart this house, you jazz singer, you," while my mother sat weeping in the corner, smashing every Yossele Rosenblatt '78 in his collection;

If only a shelfful of Talmud had caved in upon me one day, leaving my goyisher kop forever addled.

If only Tradition had barfed me forth onto the dry sands of Western civilization, I could have grown up into a big shot, a contender: a stammering, nattering, chest-pulling Jewish intellectual with nothing on my mind but social justice and yellow-haired shiksas, the hero of a thousand novels.

But on account of my sins I was pulled out of the dress rehearsal for the Major C.H. Douglas Collegiate Institute Christmas and New Year's Gala, participation compulsory if you wanted to pass music, just as I was stepping into the spotlight. Blacked up like a pair of Passover shoes, a derby hat clutched to the heart of my red vest, my payes tucked up inside a curly wig, I was in the middle of the chorus, the *solo chorus*, of *I Want A Girl (Just Like The Girl)*, when into the gym comes Khaim Mes, the president of the burial society, hopping and twitching and flapping his arms, ignoring the screams of the teacher to run right up and grab me in full sight of twenty-five other giggling minstrels.

"A mission of mercy," he yelled to the teacher, then motioned me down so he could whisper in my ear. I was just gone thirteen, so addicted to pimples and hard-ons that my glands lacked the strength for growing, but Khaim barely came up to my shoulders. I shook my head. I knew what he wanted, but for once I was helpless--I'd davened at home, and this rehearsal was life or death.

Khaim was getting ready to cry. They were all Christians here, especially the teacher. An educated man, reads notes and shpilt piano--the back of the hand, the front of the boot wouldn't do. Khaim was wringing his hands, his dentures on tiptoe at the end of his tongue, while Mr. Dee, the teacher, tapped his baton and cleared his throat like a teacher. Khaim waved him off and sucked his teeth back in. He was desperate. He looked me up and down like an Orchard Street tailor, leaned forward and yanked a handful of shirt from the waist of my pin-striped pants, tugging at it with both hands until the pressure reached my neck and I had to bow before the buttons popped off.

This was my chance. Khaim had relaxed his grip and was making with his tongue like I was supposed to give bare tit. I snapped to attention, Khaim's tongue cut a stripe through my burnt-cork and greasepaint. He still hadn't uttered a word, and I smirked down as if to ask, "Whatcha gonna do about it, Jewboy?" preening myself on my regular guyness until I noticed my right front tsitse lying flush against a pin-stripe, like an arrow in the eyes of the uncircumcised.

The teacher was silent. He was the nervous type, his nose had started to bleed. Even the kids weren't laughing--Khaim was too agitated, and also too old, and most of their parents owed him money. It was up to me.

I took a giant step forward, the better to distance myself from Khaim and the chorus, pulled my stomach in, my shoulders way back, started twirling the fringe like a zoot-suit watch-chain, and burst, triumphantly, into *Got the World on a String*. What with the laughter and applause--all guaranteed, one hundred percent spontaneous--I knew I'd arrived where I was meant to be, and I don't mean a high school gym. Fuck high school. By this time next year I'd be the toast of Broadway, the chocolate- covered matse of my people's aspirations. Mere coincidence that I, too, was the son of a cantor? That I, too, was starting out in blackface, that I'd seen *The Jolson Story* seventeen times? Vus far a tsifal, a kavincidents? Every Chanuka and Dominion Day, whether you liked it or not--and who couldn't like it? It was good for the Jews; whether you'd seen it or not--and who hadn't seen it? Who was it, wasn't going to shul, wouldn't give a couple of bucks to help support our institutions? Every summertime and winter, whether we were suffering from hayfever or catarrh: special, one-night-only, charity'll save you from death, *THE JOLSON STORY*, in our air-conditioned, newly-renovated--didn't Khaim bring some chairs from his furniture store? And old Mrs. Grynszpan with the homemade ceramic ashtrays?--*Community Centre*! vivat, zul lebn, it' a jolly good cellar--the basement part of the shul, right next to the mikve used only by my parents and Khaim's wife, Shmiley's mother and the dead (Monday and Friday, men; Tuesday and Thursday, women and dishes; corpses on demand): *The Jolson Story* and a second great hit, all proceeds to the synagogue and Israeli orphans. *The Jolson Story* and *Sword in the Desert*. *The Jolson Story* and *Yankel der Shmid*. *The Jolson Story* and *Grine Felder*, that classic of rustic yiddishkayt whose author once lived in Calgary and had even married a local girl in 1919. Twice a year, every year, since I don't know when--it's no wonder I was already farJolsont in gantsn.

And by the time I hit "I'm in love," the last line of the chorus, I realized that I was: with show-biz and lights and the unquestioning approbation of people I didn't like; with myself out-front and my destiny; and, just to be on the safe side, with God Almighty and His holy Torah, with the mishne, the gemore, the mourners of Zion, the students of the sages and the Hebrew Actors' Union. O, shoot me a shadkhn for Hedy Lamarr, I'm thirteen years old and ready to fly. Hear my voice, O Lord--it's ok, don't worry, I take requests.

I was paralyzed with exultation. The kids were all clapping, Khaim's face was covered with tears, even the teacher was shooting me a thumbs-up with the hand that wasn't pinching his nose. By them it was practically meshiekhs tsaytn, but what did they know? My beulah land was yonder, garbed as a cowgirl in the girls' gym, practising *Pistol Packin' Mama*. Since I walked into her house right after she moved down from Calgary--she was one of the new Jewish girls Shmiley took me to meet--and saw her standing in the kitchen in white knee-socks, her hair pulled back, eating Cheez treyfene Whiz straight from the jar and smiling shyly to meet me--bits of Cheez Whiz cleaving piously to her braces--from that second on, the rest of my life was nothing but commentary. The Lord was my shepherd, my father was my father, but Sabina Mandelbroit was It--a Jewish girl with the brains of Einstein and the breasts of Phryne. My bowels were stirred and refused to come to rest. Pustules conquered my cheeks, I suffered from strange upset stomachs. An afflatus rose within me, fueled by the Song of Songs: "Your braces are like a mirror of Solomon, no chewing gum has dulled their surface." I would have left father and mother to get to her, I would've given God a raincheck. To win the heart of Sabina Mandelbroit, I would have bitten off my tongue, passed it through the fire to Moloch and sent the ashes to Father Divine.

Jolson rescued me within a week. I must have walked by her house six hundred and thirteen times already, pretending not to see her, when Sabina came out on the second of July, one day after we'd watched *The Jolson Story* from opposite ends of the same room, and asked if I was walking maybe downtown. It was all I could do to grunt. All I can remember is getting down on one knee in the soda shop next to Louie Yankelovitch's movie theatre--I was drinking water from a take-out cup--and gazing over the top of a tulip glass into the glorious face of Sabina Mandelbroit herself. "There's only one way to tell you how I feel," I said, and I gave her the chorus to *Banks of the Wabash*--the only part they sang in the movie--then stood up and announced, "My name is Asa Yoelson and I love you. I sing with my father in the synagogue...Oy, the synagogue!" and out I ran, like Asa from the burlesque house, throwing a whole dollar bill at the table and not even looking to see where it landed: What if she was laughing 'cause I looked like a jerk? I groaned under Yankelovitch's marquee, pretending to chain-smoke, for almost twenty minutes. Finally she came out, limping a little and without her knee-socks. She took my hand. She spoke. "They made me clean up the puddle, you bastard."

Her sister put out for Shmiley--"Hairy tits," he told me--and they never spoke again. We didn't know from putting out; we used to smooch on the weekends, when her parents went to Calgary for cultural pursuits. They were in Calgary and we were in the basement, just the two of us and her father's Piaf records. I wouldn't turn off the lights or touch the record player--God, it was a sin already to listen, shabbes--but I knew I was just as guilty as she was...She'd, uh, take off her blouse if I let her wear my yarmulke. An eye for an eye, a tooth for a tooth, quid pro quo or something out of nothing? I don't know; all I know is we were in each other's arms, half-clothed and dreaming, her breasts cupped under my hands, my payes atwirl in her fingers...

And I sighed there in the spotlight, amid the laughter and applause, the nudging, murmured acknowledgments that maybe I wasn't such a crankshaft after all--I stood there and sighed, trying to recall some psalm of thanksgiving for all the numberless goodly benefactions of God and His Jolie, when Khaim Mes took advantage of the quiet and ran up to me again, pulled my head down by the ear, pressed his forehead to my cheek and shouted up into my eyeballs, "Your father, in the shul, dead." And I was so well trained, I didn't even blink. It came out like the air from a bellows. "Barukh dayan emes, blessed be the true judge." Then I went cold. There were black lines around everything, like in stained glass windows. Khaim caught me by the sleeve and we dragged off home.

It was the first full day of Chanuka; my father had gone to shul early to set up chairs for the evening's show. He was planning to close the store that afternoon--the first time he hadn't done so for God--so that he and my mother could come see me in the Gala, then eat an early supper and hurry back to the shul for a quick daven and a brand new second feature, *Ketskill Hunyemun*. Not only were we lucky enough to have Chanuka and Christmas Eve coincide that year, so that we didn't have to sit home wishing we had a television and refusing to study--no way the Yoizele was gonna pick up any points from our learning--but how many men who sleep in their kupls ever get to watch their sidelocked heirs in the non-sectarian part of the Christmas pageant? O Kanade, iz dus a land?--I hadn't told him about *Jolly St. Nick* or *The Christmas Song.* My father finished with the chairs, went upstairs to daven--Sabina's father had yortsayt and was springing for a decent kiddish--and then dropped dead with his tefillin half-way up his arm.

Khaim couldn't understand it. My father had never been sick a day in his life, and what had we come here for, except to stay alive? This wasn't supposed to happen. Problems, yeah, sure, everybody had problems--mir zenen dekh yidn, huh?--but except for Khazkel Baalebos going up for real-estate fraud and paying Meyer Goldenberg to take the rap, so it all worked out, anyway--except for that, which you can hardly count, the sorrows of the new world, insofar as it was framed by Coalbanks, Alberta, had been as short and as soft as a baby. Family troubles vanished, business problems passed, things came, things went, but borukh-a-shem, things could always be worse.

So what the hell was going wrong? "Forty-one years old," Khaim was screaming, "A head of iron and a heart of gold, and God, may He be Blessed, throws it all to the worms? They need him up there so badly?" Khaim was pointing to the heavenly yeshiva. "Rabbi Akiva wants his opinion on the poro adumeh, the red heifer, so the widow and the orphan just bar-mitzvah have to go look out for themselves? Where is the judgment? And where's the judge?" He shot me a look like I knew but wouldn't tell. "How many years atone for nothing?"

I knew better than to try and answer. He was dragging me along like a pull-toy, tossing our hands into the air every so often to crown me heavyweight champion of the world. "A man born and raised and completely absorbed in holiness can't live to see his only son get married? Is this what our sins have brought us? Then let God punish the sinners." Khaim jerked his chin skyward. "He protects the widow and the orphan? Avadeh, of course He does--only first He sits down and creates them." He sniffed, and wiped his nose with my sleeve. "Ay, Yoinele, you and me, we're like two sides of the same coin"--God forbid--"the two most miserable creatures on earth."

I wanted to know where he fit in. I was thinking of what he'd called me--yusem, orphan--and I could see what was coming if I didn't change the subject. My father hadn't been gone more than twenty minutes or half an hour, and already

Khaim was starting. Forget whose picture they'd been using to raise money, Khaim couldn't think of anything but Khaim. "You're a son without a father," he was saying. "And I, I'm a father without a son--worse than without," he added.

"Khaim," I said. I had to stop him before it was too late; I'd never called him by his first name before, and I was hoping it'd bring him around. "Zug mir, Khaim, 'kh bin takeh a yusem, I'm really an orphan?" I still didn't feel like one. "Er iz takeh, he's really--?" Khaim stopped in mid-stride and unbuttoned his coat. He pulled me to him as if to give me suck. "Got vet er mer nisht loybn," he said. "He'll praise God no more."

I bit my lip and took it like a man. Khaim folded me under his arms in a double headlock, my head and shoulders buttoned up inside his coat and my tukhes exposed to the prairie wind. My name might be Jonasz in English, but if *Pinocchio* was any indication, I'd rather have been swallowed by a whale than been locked up inside Khaim's winter coat. The stink of mothballs and sweat in there, the taste of his shirt between my teeth, the bounce bounce bounce of my head against his chest--I was carsick already. He smoked cigars from my father's store, three for a dime, and he stank like a club-car. I couldn't tell any more whether my tears were from terror or the stench. My lips and teeth were covered with the residue of my make-up, and the rest of Al Jolson was on Khaim's white shirt.

"He protects the widow and the orphan?" Khaim was shouting down his collar like I'd tried to steal his dick. I started to giggle in spite of myself. Call him Khaim? I might as well have called him mister. I could have lost ten fathers, the shirt off my back, anything but my cherry, and Khaim, good old Khaim, would still be saying kaddish for himself.

His wife died in 1940, a heart attack. "You understand now what this means?" Since she'd had rheumatic fever back in the old country, her health had been nothing to write home about. "And how could I have written?" he wanted to know. To her family, to his family, where they were, if they were, heart failure was a pinch in the cheek.

Then his son came home from the army. Had to come home. Singing and rubbing his thing, slurping his gob and making bubbles with it. Something blew up too close to his head, oys medical student.

What could you do? Khaim moped around for a few weeks-
-"God should forgive me, I felt sorrier for myself than I did for
the boy"--then gave out with a nebekh and a shrug and put the
kid to work. He could still mop floors in Khaim's furniture
store, dust the stock, get his father from the back. And if it
wasn't the Mayo Clinic, it wasn't the broom factory, either.

"Why me?" Nobody knew. Khaim was a good man, a nice
guy, very pious. Not even the oldest of the old men, the snuff-
shmeckers and earhorn addicts who sat around figuring God's
balance of punishments, could come up with any reason.
Khaim Mes owned two hundred pieces of furniture, prayed
three times a day, and even put up the money for a mikve so
that he and the late Hinde could live in Coalbanks as husband
and wife. Khaim Mes didn't deserve this.

And what happened next--Job himself shouldn't know.
Khaim was dying of loneliness and grief. Dave, the boy, was
more than a handful. He ran around town like a Cossack in a
sukke--tanked up, singing filthy army songs, forgetting that it
was illegal to piss in the street. "I'm embarrassed even to
remember," Khaim said. He wasn't evil or foolish, the boy, the
way you usually think of malice or folly; he was just a bundle
of inclinations with nothing left to bend. He needed a mother.

So Khaim wrote a few letters and got him one. "There were
plenty of D.P.'s, God preserve us, in 1946," plenty of women
with no living relatives looking for a way out of Europe. Khaim
knew what he wanted and found it: mid- to late thirties,
previously married, religiously observant, and willing and able
to look after a war hero who was no longer quite with
everything. Physical description appreciated, photograph not
required.

Khaim made all the arrangements and set out to meet her
in Calgary. He wanted to look her over, to marry her and have
a little pleasure without Dave getting in the way. So he left the
boy on Faivel Potasznik's farm--too much trouble he couldn't
get into out there--and stood on the platform, just like in the
movies, holding a sign with the woman's name on it in Jewish.

"I thought God was finally through with me." He had his
eye out for a baalebuste straight from the gooseyard, but what
came up and asked, "Efsher zent ets Misteh Shpilkover?"--this
was "a verse from the Song of Songs." Tall, lithe, swelling like

the sea even under her long-sleeved, modest dress; her hair under the kerchief like the straps on a bar-mitzvah boy's tefillin. And Khaim, for once, found himself happy to think impurely.

When they went to get Dave, they found him up to his knees in cowpies and happy. Khaim and Faivel--they were landsmen from Radom--worked out a deal: Dave would stay on at the farm and Faivel would send his pay to Khaim. Every Sunday, the newlyweds drove out to visit.

Now comes the good part. To me, Mrs. Khaim was an old lady already. She was probably about thirty-five when all this happened--my mother wasn't thirty-five--but everybody said that she was really some looker when she first got here, you could imagine what she must have been like before. Anyway, Dave came into town for the holidays. He never quite grasped just who this woman was supposed to be, and Yom Kippur in the afternoon, between musaf and minkhe while Khaim was dozing in shul, he made a grab for his father's wife. Half her dress came off in his hand, and she made for the street, naked and screaming. On Yom Kippur, yet. Some neighbours took her in, and Mrs. Khaim had never been so thankful that she could speak Ukrainian.

"Ay-yay-yay, yay-yay, yay-yay. The voice is the voice of Jacob," and Khaim's was that of our Social Credit premier's Sunday Bible-readings on the radio; he was getting ready to hit you with the khidesh, the brilliant new interpretation he'd been working on all week and that his wife, the Mrs. Social Credit Premier, was so proud of that she was sitting at home beside their pre-war Atwater Kent, squirming in her overstuffed wing-chair, or whatever it is that cultured goyim like that keep in their living rooms--their parlours--and I couldn't even shut him off. This was a whole new deal. "Ay-yay-yay" was the end of the story, you could ask anybody. He'd ay-yay-yay, maybe do it again if he was in a good mood, khork around for some phlegm in his throat and give a good green spit. That was always the final amen, the new suit and ten-dollar bill that meant you were free, and whatever this Bible stuff was, I didn't like it. I'd been sick of this story for years, and I could hardly even breathe inside of his coat. It was cold and slippery and we couldn't stay in step--I was doubled over almost triple, my knees practically touching my chest, and Khaim was busy asking me what Rashi, the eleventh-century commentator, thought of the verse in question. I didn't know and I didn't care--I *did* know, but I didn't care--so I grunted and moved my jaws so he'd think I was talking. Khaim sighed. "Aval Eysev"--he was prompting me, chanting like a six year-old in kheyder--"Aval Eysev be-lashon kanturia diber." For about ten seconds all I could hear was the dragging of our feet, the beat of Khaim's heart, the sound of my wig bunching over my hair as my head rubbed against his chest. "Nu, Yoinele," I could tell he was exasperated, that I'd missed my cue. "Fartaytsh shoyn, translate it already."

Like I had any choice. "Ober Eysev hot harte reyd geret, he spoke like a brute." Khaim's chest took the edge off my tone.

"Good." Good is right, I thought. One of these days I'm gonna stop being such a good boy and punch you right in the false teeth. "And what do we have here? It still *sounds* like my Dovidl, but what comes out of his mouth...Ay, s'iz nisht far ka yidn gedakht, it shouldn't happen to a Jew."

That did it. Forget the suit and the bill and the pat on the back--nisht far ka yidn gedakht was the small print at the front of the catalogue, the unconditional guarantee that all the crap up ahead could be delivered at any time, from God knows where into your very own living room. Freak accidents, rashes from nowhere, children who converted to Christianity and became missionaries to the Jews--nisht far ka yidn gedakht meant it had happened to somebody else and was probably going to happen to you--you were alive, weren't you? You could define a Jew's whole life by what shouldn't happen to him--shouldn't happen to him again--and I didn't have any time for the ghost of tsuris past. "And from your mouth, Khaim?" I asked, craning my neck towards the tailor's label on his inside pocket. "What comes out of *it*?" He would have given me a look, if he could have. "Your own sorrows give you licence to fardrey, to distort, the Holy Torah? Where are the hands of Esau, you empty vessel, you?"

It was the rudest I'd ever been to an adult Jew. Khaim stopped and relaxed his grip. The coat was rising along my cheek, tightening over my neck. He'd spread his arms, lifted them over his head so he could beat me and crack my nape like I was a scoffer's ass. No wonder we needed a fence around the Torah.

His coat was darker than ever, there was an inside button caught on my ear, but my life wasn't flashing before my eyes. "Bless ye the Lord, Who is to be blessed!" He was davening, for God's sake. His hands came down and he grabbed me all over again, even tighter. "The voice of Jacob? The voice of Shaye himself; your father's voice and very words. Shaye Levkes would never suffer me to talk like the fool I am, and neither will his son. You're absolutely right, Yoinele, there's no fool like an old fool. And you wanna know who is the biggest fool? Eh? The kind of shoyteh ben pik-holts, the dimwit ben woodpecker who sweeps his troubles into the face of an orphan."

He started aying and yaying all over again, like the little engine that could on Yom Kippur, building steam for the journey ahead. He shuffled, he puffed, his paunch rolled forward and off we went, with me edging nearer to deadweight all the time. Just when I'd got so sick of him and his kvetching that I was nearly back to normal--or as normal as you can get when your father's just died and you're hopping around like Quasimodo in a coatful of somebody else--Khaim had to go and say it again, this time with hair-oil. It was bad enough when he called me an orphan, but "the face of an orphan"? God help me, it sounded like a Yiddish movie, the one they were really going to be showing that night, right down to the hairy frames and popping sound, the disordered reels that nobody'd even notice as I spilled off the screen and onto the walls, a reject extra from the cast of *Boys' Town* with TB cheeks and an out-sized cap--my sole patrimony--hawking in nasal plainchant: "Cigarettes, matchsticks; kaylekhdik azoy, un fest un git gepakt, so round, so firm, so fully-packed: Y.L.M.L.O., Y.L.M.L.O.--that's right, Yoine Levkes Means Living Orphan..."

And as the leaves flake like dandruff from the Home of the Sages of Israel Perpetual Jewish Holiday Calendar Until the Messiah Should Come Speedily and In Our Day, as the angel choir hoists its burden on the war-amps soundtrack and old Mr. Morgenstern in the audience pulls the horn from his ear and asks, "Vuddehel mit de screamin?"--I come stumbling at last, mortgage money in hand, into the little brown shack, the cottage for sale, the house I live in, where my doubly bereaved and sole remaining parent lies sucking her shoelaces, trying to guess the anniversary of my death. "Mama!" I cry. She stops chewing long enough to give a look at my prematurely wise and fatherless visage, the snow from the non-stop Canadian storm melting in torrents through my endless payes; she sits up in her sickbed, speaks in a voice tinged with maggots and dirt. "It'd kill you to put on a coat?" and promptly drops dead, the end.

They'd cry themselves silly. The floor of the Community Centre would be a pilgrim shrine of hernia trusses, hair pieces, the alte Mrs. Reingewirtz's new glass eye with the Israeli flag in the pupil--free-will offerings for my brand new pushcart. I'd get an Oscar for insult and injury, fallen women would send me fan mail, I'd make a fortune from residuals and licensing fees: The Yoine Levkes Living Orphan Doll--with detachable crutch: press its stomach and hear it kvetch. Throw away your hula hoops, I don't read *Time Magazine* for nothing.

I was nuts already, shikker with dolour and stink. Khaim was bewailing something or other, we were tripping and sliding worse than ever, and none of it hurt any more. I was pixilated, having mirages. I said hello to Silvana Mangano and she handed me a piece of herring. It tasted like Khaim, and it offered a suggestion. I'd just worked up the nerve to ask him to will his coat to a dentist's office, when I heard the trickle of a little brook from inside his shirt. There was nothing I could do but wait.

Talk about the luck of the Irish--one third of my people was gone, there was a peat fire burning all round me, and I couldn't even sing *Mavourneen*--it would have meant having to breathe. Khaim had come out with a wet one, a low plopper that could have stopped a regiment in the trenches and was twisting around my throat like last year's dickey. I was purple under the blackface, blaspheming and afraid to inhale--how many years breathing gallnuts atone for nothing? I hated God, I hated Khaim, forever, for b.o., for what the two of them were doing to me. I wanted to vault from Khaim's coat like a cock out of longjohns and head straight for trouble, *my kind of trouble*, counting the oymer in Roman numerals kind of trouble. I could see myself in an apron and chef's hat, seething a kid in its mother's milk--with Quik and Bosco syrup--to raise money for the shul. Let em eat treyf, they already did, see if I care. It was God's turn to squirm and I was gonna teach Him what it was to be impotent. If I could only get out of Khaim's coat, I'd light such a fire under His ass, He'd shit barbecue from now until Shavues.

Khaim didn't even excuse himself. He was too busy yelling down his collar about filial duties and honouring the memory and looking after mom and how I wasn't a kid anymore, and I couldn't lift an arm to plug my nose. I wanted to bite him in the pipik, french-kiss it and spit his greenhorn lint at every mom and god and goy and khaim there was. Everything's in the hands of heaven except the fear of heaven, and by the time I got hit, I was thinking only in dirty words. I jerked upright with a manic twitch, popping Khaim's buttons and slamming my skull so hard into his chin that he damn near lost his tongue. I was too startled to be stunned; I grabbed my tukhes and started wheeling out of Khaim's coat, and caught another one on the tip of my nose. They'd put rocks in the snowballs, the pricks, and I started bleeding right away, the second nosebleed I'd seen that morning.

All of a sudden I had real enemies, Bruce Wohlgelernter and Stevie Gurfein, a couple of yidn, naturally, and two of the biggest potunks in town. They obviously hadn't heard the news.

"Hey, look, it's the Levkes pisher. Havin a good daven down there?" Brucie was laughing.

"You think he can mumble with his mouth full?" Stevie asked. "Let's give im seconds."

I was after them before they finished packing the snow, sliding over the ice in my bloodstained and spotty blackface like some sort of avenging Eliza from *Uncle Tom's Cabin*. "Cocksucker pigshit fucks," I was screaming. "I'll kill the fuckin botha ya." Khaim was right behind me. "He protects the widow and the orphan? Phooey! Me, Khaim, I protect them. Keep running, pogromtchikes! If I catch you, the Angel of Death'll be hanging his laundry from your kishkes."

Nu, riddle me jerk-offs. They had to have recognized Khaim from in front--no way they'd have tried this on a goy-- but at the sight of a running grown-up who knew their parents, they dropped their half-made snowballs and took off in opposite directions. Khaim went after Stevie and I slipped on the ice. The Lord, however, was quick to forgive--or maybe He just wanted to butter me up--and he slid me right into Wohlgelernter's legs, bringing him down on his backside. I fell over his chest and began pounding my fist into his throat. I'd picked this up in a detective novel. Punching him in the face might hurt, might even draw blood, but I wanted to kill. "Fuck with me, will ya," and my fist slammed into his Adam's apple. His eyes bugged out, his tongue was staggering across his lips like a drunk on Saturday night. His mouth was wide open, but he couldn't get his wind. His breath smelled like my grandmother's armpits. "Tumour!" I screamed, punching him again. "You bloody fuckin tumour-cunt!"

He'd have killed me if he could have stopped gagging. Calling him Tumour when he was around was like calling kids with polio Hoppy, and not even an idiot likes to be reminded that the fruit don't fall too far from the tree--Brucie was a regular graft of his parents...

Every doctor she saw told Mrs. Wohlgelernter that the oven was bunless, there was a growth in her gut; even after she had to give up typing and her locally famous ankles looked like they had a toothache. And the goddamned thing kept growing. Go tell her that the doctors were crazy, they were too busy playing Jean Hersholt to have any idea about anything, that she should go up to Calgary and see a specialist--no matter what anybody said, Sylvia Wohlgelernter proclaimed her absolute faith in the doctors of Coalbanks; they brought *her* into the world, didn't they?

She never wrote her husband about it. He was busy invading Europe and had plenty to think about. A sick wife would just depress him, maybe even alienate his affections. So when she wrote to say ha ha, guess what, she'd been sick but not really and they now had a nine pound baby boy, Benny Wohlgelernter was ready to throw himself in front of a V-2. They'd only had one night together before he went--Benny was afraid she might marry Lenny Nightingale's brother, who moved to Toronto and became a lawyer--there'd been no sign of a tumour when he went away, and here he was all of a sudden a father, why should he believe it? Especially since the letter was dated a month after the birthday. He spent every spare moment for the next four years boozing and whoring, sending his wife detailed descriptions of her "sisters over the sea." He had nothing to live for, and came home with the Distinguished Service Cross and a chestful of other fruit salad.

The Mrs., meanwhile, was more upset by his attempts to get himself killed than by his silly suspicions. She didn't exactly enjoy his letters, but she had a whole town to vouch for her, and after a couple of years it was clear to everybody that the kid was a miniature double of Benny, right down to the sloping forehead and double chin. She knew he'd stopped reading her letters when Benny didn't respond to the pictures. And when he dragged his dejected ass off the train and took one look at that little caveman of a tumour, Benny burst into tears and started kissing Sylvia's knees right there in the station, begging her forgiveness.

Nobody ever forgot, though; the little boy was still known as "Oh, you mean *The Tumour*," even in Yiddish. You just couldn't say it around the Wohlgelernters: Sylvia would burst into tears; Benny would try and take you out like a machine gun nest; and The Tumour himself would either sulk away, tell you to fuck off or beat the living shit out of you, depending on your size. He was a senior at Major Douglas, and they said he didn't shower after gym. Nobody his age paid him any attention, so he went around bothering younger kids, in company with Stevie Gurfein, his only friend, a practical joker with a face like a French tickler. The Red Menace, they called him at school. Shmiley and a couple of goyim once dunked his head in a toilet after they'd all taken leaks, 'cause he'd given Shmiley some diarrhea gum.

They must have had a fair idea whose ass was sticking out of Khaim's middle--how many other kids hung out with the old men?--and even if they didn't, they could still have had a good giggle, sitting in the cafeteria and trading snot sandwiches.

I was bouncing up and down on The Tumour's chest, blood and blackface running over my chin, my shirt like the inside of a bandage. At every twitch of his shoulder, I'd crack him across the throat. "Prick! Fuckface! Tumour! You ever so much as look at me again, *dickweed*, you or your shit-for-brains pimple-friend, you'll be sittin on your shoulders the rest of your life, understand?" I bent over and rubbed my shirt across his mouth; got up, screwed my heel into his nuts a couple of times and left him in a puking heap.

Sic semper beheymes. My nose was bleeding, my father was dead, it was ten below zero and my coat was at school, but I was feeling so good that I didn't even bother to look back at the prostrate Tumour. I'd always said I could live if they'd let me, and I was starting to make them let me--*now* I wanted to eat a great big steak and then get laid, even if it *was* a quarter to nine in the morning and I was staring into the sun and pinching my nostrils to try and stop the bleeding. Khaim and Stevie had disappeared, and I was finally fulfilling my father's dream, the one he'd never confided to me, but that I knew from all the commentaries was what every father wants for his son. I was doing what he had never done, what he'd never been able to do: I was doing what I wanted, instead of what passed for a yid. If only Wohlgelernter had been a goy; if only I'd killed him instead of wracking him up; if only I'd known what it was like to get laid, I would have been Misha Mlotek in I, the Jewry.

I'd been working towards it, consciously, ever since I started going with Sabina Soon as we got together, people--teachers, even--started looking at me with new respect. "Little fucker must be hung like a horse," I heard someone in another gym class once say; otherwise she'd be going out with one of the hip j.d.'s or the guys with the turtlenecks on the school magazine. Sabina was the hottest piece in any three grades, and all of a sudden girls stopped pulling my payes and started to look at me...in that way. All of a sudden I stopped taking shit, especially from teachers, especially from geniuses like our English teacher, who had us read *Oliver Twist* and *The Merchant of Venice* one right after the other, not just us but all the other freshmen, too--probably some Social Credit fringe benefit--and then had the khutspe to send me to the principal when I came into class one day with my payes hanging down, a fake beard looped over my ears, mumbling and muttering as I went through everyone's pockets. I'd cooked it up with Shmiley, and we let Sabina and Greg Ramsay in on it. Ramsay's pompadour and Cuban heels were both three inches high, but he was kind of a friend of Shmiley, from Shmiley's other friends, the ones who never bothered to kick me because I wasn't worth the effort. Once Ramsay let me into his pockets, I could go into anybody's, and when the old bitch came into the room and asked what I thought I was doing in *her* class, I gave her my best

Hyman Kaplan voice and said, "Ya dunno, lady? I'm de youngster from di Elders from Zion, and I'm looking here for a pound flesh."

I told the principal that Mrs. Nolan's choice of reading material, or perhaps it was the Board of Education's, was making me the butt of prejudiced jokes and getting me into fights on my way home from school--like it had never happened before. Not only that, but she'd forced me, *me*, to read "Hath not a Jew eyes..." in front of the whole class. He told me to apologize; I told him to tell Shakespeare and Charles Dickens to apologize, and if they wouldn't listen, then he should tell Mrs. Nolan or we'd use her blood for day-old matses. I was kicked out of English for a couple of days, but the idea finally soaked through. Instead of *Ivanhoe*, we got to read poems that didn't say anything about anybody, only daffodils and dead birds and minstrel boys and corners that'd always be England, and Mrs. Nolan hadn't acknowledged my hand since.

Not that the principal was such a guardian of Israel or anything; he'd already assigned me to a social worker, and she was the one who got him to give in: I was such an adjustment problem already, why go looking for trouble? I'd been seeing her twice a week almost every week that fall, while the rest of the school was eating lunch or cheering our teams. They worked it that way on purpose, my parents shouldn't know, 'cause they figured my parents were most of the problem. Nu, give a goy a brain, he might lose the sponge from his bathtub. They were worried--herst, worried--I was missing too much school on account of Jewish holidays that as far as they were concerned were nisht geshtoygn un nisht gefloygn, castles in the air that couldn't even float. Rosh Hashana, Yom Kippur, all right. But what the hay was this Sukkes, this Tabernacles?

"This Succoth," the senior gym teacher doubled as freshman guidance counsellor, "Sounds to me like suck-off. Sounds to me like jerk-off. Sounds to me like you got your hands in your pockets, Levkes. Well, at Major Douglas, you're gonna grab your socks, you know what I mean, four-eyes?"

"Mr. Curtis," you fat fuck, "I don't wear glasses."

"Well, you should, beany boy, you should." Keep it up, shit-for-brains, they'll find you burned in your bunker. "Lissename, Levkes. Except for the War, I been at Major

Douglas since Jesus was a lance-corporal, and I never heard a *anybody* takin off on Suck-off, and believe me, Levkes, there's been plenty of you people passed through here already. Your New Year's, your Fast Day, all right; nobody's beefin you get our New Year's, too--but you want four *more* days--I thought you people loved education."

"If you don't believe me, Mr. Curtis, please call my parents." I had nothing more to say. "Now. I'd like to get back to English. It's my favourite class." I let my wrist hang loose somewhere around my shoulder.

"That doesn't surprise me." Prick-on-wheels called them then and there. He got off the phone, sniffing for fresh meat. "I think they said it was ok. From what I could make out." He looked at my file. "Says here, Levkes, that you're a Chinaman."

"I was born in Shanghai, if that's what you mean."

He raised his eyebrows.

"Sir," I added.

"You don't look like no Chinaman. Fong didn't ask for time off." Darius Fong was one of the few ok guys in my class; his father ran The Number One Son Chinese and Canadian Cuisine downtown.

"We were refugees. My parents went there from Poland. To escape from the Germans."

"So you didn't belong there, either. And what about Greenberg?"

"He was born in Russia. His parents escaped there."

"I don't give a sh--darn where he was born. How come he isn't asking?"

"He'll take it sick. Come back with a note."

"Clever. And why don't you?"

I was losing control. Fast. "For the same reason I wear a beany and curls, *sir*. I don't feel it necessary, *sir*," the asshole was still a teacher, "To ask your forgiveness for what I am, or to ask your permission to be that way." I'd been working on this speech all summer, just in case, and was almost happy to get the chance to use it.

"Well, you know, Levkes, it's against the rules here to wear hats in class. It isn't a synagogue. And it's my job to enforce the rules."

"They let me wear it at Aberhart," where I'd gone until grade eight. "Once my parents explained, they even let me wear a baseball hat so I wouldn't look too weird."

"Well, this isn't Aberhart, and you better take that thing off. Now."

"I'm sorry, sir, but it's against my religion to go around bareheaded."

"Now, Levkes."

"My father told me, sir, that only the wind or a fist should ever take it off."

"Are you defying me, Levkes?" Mr. Curtis leaned over his desk and blew me a kiss. I stared him down. "Looks like the fist, Levkes." He got up, straightened his shoulders and pulled in his gut--The Vat, everybody called it; there was a big brewery in Coalbanks--then came around and put his hand on my head, cupping it over my yarmulke.

"You've got hair like a girl, too." He tweaked a paye. "Now, do you take it off or do I?" He clawed at the kupl, collapsing it towards the middle. "Here it goes, boy. No one gets special consideration here."

I felt like I'd just been kicked in the balls. Teachers were supposed to stop people from doing this. "If you don't stop that, sir, I'll have to tell the principal that you assaulted me." Curtis was said to have once hit a *teacher* who dared to disagree with him in public.

He laughed. "Don't fuck with me, Abie."

The space between my elbow and his gut was so short, he never saw it coming. The bastard was all flab. "You ever lay a hand on me again, you Social Credit Schickelgruber, I'll tell em you locked me in here and blew me 'til I came bone marrow." I was about half-sure what this meant, but I knew damn well it'd drive him up the wall.

"You little shit." I threw myself on the floor, banged my head against the corner of the desk a couple of times--I had to make it look good--kicked over the garbage can and screamed as loud as I could, "I'll take it off, I'll take it off. Just please don't kick me any more, Mr. Curtis."

Two secretaries, a guidance counsellor and one of the vice-principals came running in. The men restrained Mr. Curtis while the secretaries looked at my wounds, then we all had an emergency meeting with the principal. Curtis was warned about never touching a student; I got the as-a-believer-in-the-Old-Testament-you-should-know-better-than-to-bear-false-witness routine. "I could expel you, Levkes, for lying like that. Why, I could expel you for the language you used--obscenity and sedition are both illegal in this country," and he wanted me to know that many a member of the Social Credit Party had given his life for "your people" in the late War. Between my birthplace and my appearance, he was probably worried that I was passing hockey scores to the Russians. "But I think you need help. You've got to learn to adjust to society." If I agreed to see a social worker, he, the principal, wouldn't tell my parents about this incident with Mr. Curtis. And I wasn't to tell anybody about the social worker; if the principal had to explain her, I would have to be punished.

So I lied to everybody more than usual and started meeting with Miss Dehmel at the beginning of October. My parents would never have known, anyway--to tell them we got off for football games would have meant having to go home early and do more gemore--but Shmiley and Sabina were a little more difficult. I told them I was doing more extra Latin. I'd taken to the stuff like an anas to aqua; I'd been so scared by the idea of it, a fear reinforced by Sabina's older sister, Genia, who said it was completely impossible, that I got hold of the textbook over the summer and started to work my way through it. Remember, in a frum household sleeping 'til seven is already mid-afternoon, so I had plenty of time to kill before Sabina could come out to play. I did a lesson a day, shokling over the Latin book like it was some kind of Tractate, running the fringes of my tsitsis through my fingers and muttering, "Res rei rei rem re. Festina lente," in the same chant as I used to ask the fir kashes on Pesakh. I finished the book in a month, and started to swear over the supplementary readings--"Namque me silva lupus in Sabina." This stuff made gemore look like dental floss; bastards not only destroyed the Temple and made sure I'd end up having to live in Coalbanks, but they couldn't even talk in order. Even Yiddish didn't jump around that much. Conjugavi, declinavi, parsedokowski and construedarooni until I was so tsekokht and tsemisht I started staying up nights trying to figure out what the fuck kind of verb gave a preterite like floogie from *Flat Foot Floogie*, and then I get to school and find out the book's supposed to last for the next two years, Amerike goniff. Mr. Sherbowits made me stay after class one day and recite "Egredere aliquando ex urbe", while he sighed like an old man with a glass of tea. "You seem very precocious, Levkes. You did all this over the summer, for your own enjoyment?" I was in love with every macron; what was I supposed to do, sit in the store and count gumballs while my father invented new stringencies?   Candies lead to dentistry; magazines to optometrists; aimless strolling to the shoemaker and mixed dancing to the maternity ward--shut up, kid, and keep counting. I told him I had nothing else to do. "I'm not what you'd call a social butterfly." I thought he'd like that; I couldn't imagine a Latin teacher ever having any friends.

He tried to kick me up to a grade eleven Latin class, but the principal was opposed to special consideration.   So Mr. Sherbowits gave me special reading assignments--translate and hand in--and met with me once a week after school to explain my mistakes, fix up my pronunciation--I must have been the only kid in the history of the language to recite dactylic hexameter with a Yiddish lilt--and instruct me in the finer points of the genitive of separation. Sabina thought I was crazy for liking Latin so much, but I explained to her that I wanted to make her a present with it: every line of Latin with the word sabina in it, so she'd know how famous she was.

And still I felt guilty. If Miss Dehmel, the social worker, had been Jewish, they'd have called her Miss-Dehmel-Rif-Mikh-Peggy, Miss-Dehmel-Call-Me-Peggy; to call her Miss Dehmel to her face was like telling her that she wasn't your friend. And who wouldn't want to be her friend? She was a regular pocket Venus, that Miss Dehmel, in a form-fitting skirt and top, the worst possible social worker for a kid like me. She was always touching my arm--I used to roll up my sleeves before I went in--and when she put her hand on my shoulder, and I don't mean from behind, it was strictly yodelaiehoo, I'm at the Matterhorn's tip, another half-inch I'm gonna need a glass eye--it couldn't have been *all* bra.

"You seem so...angry, Joey." I told her it was the antisemitn. Whenever I mentioned Hitler, she crossed her legs; if I wanted to see any more, I had to tell her that I felt inadequate in the locker room, or else mention my girlfriend. She'd let her breath out then, her left ankle would uncoil from around her right calf, and she'd sit there, her legs slightly parted, while I dropped my books, my pencil, my yarmulke, my wristwatch, anything short of my pants.

Sure, I felt guilty. I really did have a girlfriend and she really did have a father a psychiatrist who'd taken a personal interest in me: I was the only kid in Coalbanks who could say anal-retentive in Yiddish. I felt terrible using Sabina and her father to get a glimpse of alien crotch, but I couldn't help myself. Sabina was my age; Miss Dehmel was a mature woman, fully developed, and I had to talk non-stop to keep from drooling. I made up complexes, tsuris, true confessions, anything to keep her off balance. I even told her I had a rabbi complex, that I felt guilty for not being a sage. "While the other kids were playing cowboys and Indians," I told her, "I was stroking an imaginary beard and inspecting my mother's poultry."

You could practically hear the bells go off in her head. She was scribbling so furiously that her pencil broke. She crossed her legs, uncrossed them; I said "Hitler complex", she crossed them back the other way, too fast, and had to go behind the desk and turn her back to me to fiddle with a garter. She managed to run her right stocking all the way down to the heel. There was no stopping me now--I told her I had nightmares: Christian babies really *were* kosher and I was going to be kicked out of the Elders of Zion Youth for not having eaten my quota. Miss Dehmel just swivelled on her high heels; she wanted to save her other stocking. I dropped my pen three times; she wasn't wearing a girdle, but she knew I was holding back. When she'd heard that I'd never been to a dance, she had a look on her face like I'd exposed my circumcision.

"Mixed dancing's forbidden," I told her. "And besides, all the big dances are on Friday night."

"So you and your young lady"--I'd concealed Sabina's name for her own protection--"have never danced together?"

"I don't know about her, but I've never even danced apart, unless you count hopping around in a circle with a scroll of the law"--at least my English was getting better--"with a scroll of the law in the middle."

This wasn't strictly true. Sabina's father had a pile of Perez Prado records, and we'd mamboed enough in her basement that I could dance like a gigolo already. Still, Miss Dehmel's left hand was sandwiched between her crossed knees, her over-bitten front teeth were riding on her lower lip; it was her way of saying, "Poor, poor diamond in the rough, child of savages, what can I do to help?" She didn't need to know that Sabina and I had even used a rubber once. Not that we went all the way or anything, but they'd just had their sofa re-covered, and Sabina knew where her father kept some under his tefillin bag. By the time I got through explaining to Miss Dehmel that no power on earth could ever induce my parents to let me go to a dance--you might as well send them an engraved invitation to Sodom and Gomorrah--she had tears in her eyes and one more ruined stocking. I was nothing but a victim of circumstance.

Yeah, I could live if they let me, all right. I started the opening pass to the mambo, caught myself--I was in mourning, after all--clamped my hand back over my nose and shuffled the rest of the way home as fast as I could, my right front tsitse beating time against my thigh.

II

"That idiot Khaim." Shmiley's Hun of a mother, the legendary Serel Efsherke, the human cement-mixer who once decked a Ukrainian railway worker with a single punch, stood screaming in the doorway, while half the Jewish women in town were busy in our kitchen and living room, tsk-tsking over fate and telling each other what to do. "He needs a road-map to wipe his ass. He told you, at least?" I nodded yes. "And it scared you so much, you had to crap all over your face...Git nor a kik, ladies. Just give a look." Serel pointed at me and my face like nobody else had noticed. "Like hand-me-down panties when you bless the new moon."

She grabbed me by the collar and ran a hand down my cheek--thank God, my nose had stopped bleeding--then frowned at her fingertips like the toilet paper'd slipped. "Nu, shoyn?" She turned her hand to the crowd and displayed her stigmata. "Wipe him off before he starts a plague."

All of a sudden, I could feel for Frank Sinatra. The women were clawing at my face, fighting over my shirt like I was an unmarked Christmas present. There were fingers in my eyes, paste-on-nails scratching blood-scabs from my nostrils and chin. She was a born ringmaster, that Serel, and unless you had a gas-mask to ward off the curses, you didn't disobey. They even tore off my wig, with the yarmulke still inside it. I threw a block at Estelle Moscoe--she sold the fingernails at mah-jongg games--and was on my knees in time to catch it.

"Un di mama--nishtu?" I asked. I'd decided to stay put for a minute or two. "My mother isn't here?" I couldn't place a single pair of ankles. Serel sent off for some cold creme, then told me she was lying down. "So's my father," I said. Serel spat in the sink and left; the ladies went back to work until she returned, balancing a half-wit image of my mother on her instep and knee. They sat her down at the kitchen table, and my mother slumped like a boiled carrot. She didn't seem to be crying; she hadn't even sighed.

"Rukhl." Serel was massaging her shoulders. "Kik nor ver s'iz, Look who it is." Serel pulled her head up by the knot in her kerchief. "You were asking for him, see?" My mother's eyes looked like plombehs, the little lead badges that mean a chicken is kosher.

"Mama." My throat felt like I'd swallowed a toothpick. I started towards her, but Serel shook her head. It was worse than I'd expected.

My mother looked at me and called me Itzik, her older brother who got killed in the War. Serel shook her, she looked again and said my name, giggling like she had a crush. She kept staring, tears running down her cheeks now; nothing else moved, not her eyelids, not even her mouth. She reached back and pulled the kerchief off her head, twisting it compulsively around her knuckles without looking at it for what could have been hours.

You could hear her tears flow. Except for me and Serel, who was also the mikve lady, nobody still alive had ever seen my mother's hair--and I couldn't remember what it looked like. I probably hadn't seen it since we left Shanghai. Not first thing in the morning, not in the middle of the night when I had an earache or a bad dream--my mother slept in some kind of nightcap. She bared her head in the shower and the mikve. And maybe when they did it. But here it was, for the first time that I could really remember, thick and black, twisted and braided into circles over each of her ears, kind of like life-rafts made of khaleh--pull a button and they'd inflate to full size. It must have hung past her hips when she undid it, and I finally knew why she was always in the bathroom.

She went on staring, unravelling the kerchief and balling it into her mouth. Then she decided to speak. Whatever she was saying, it had a strange rise and fall, like Chinese gemore-niggen played on 16. The ladies started arguing--it was curses, it was Psalms, it was a charm to keep me alive. The ladies knew from nothing. My mother cooked and cleaned and worked in the store; she was always listening to the radio, and I was willing to bet everything I had that what she was really saying--go ahead, do me something; my mother *liked* those Yiddish movies--what she was really saying was, "Let your hair down and cry." I couldn't even *talk* when Johnny Ray was on.

"Tsufridn?" Serel asked me. "You happy?" I stood there like a plasticene golem while my mother started humming *The Little White Cloud That Cried*. Serel put her into a full-nelson and steered her back to the bedroom. "Don't worry," somebody said in English. "Dr. Mandelbroit sent over some tranquilizers. Really, she's all right."

I didn't have the strength to argue. "Somebody phoned already to Calgary." It was the same voice, and I still couldn't place it. "The rabbi's driving right down, so it'll be this afternoon, meerschaum." You're supposed to bury the dead as fast as you can, but I couldn't see what pipes had to do with it.

"Mirshem," somebody echoed--go talk Jewish with these people--"God willing."

"Khaim already called the khevra kaddisha," Mrs. Khaim was speaking Yiddish, "And if Dr. Mandelbroit can mirshem poyel by the antisemitn they shouldn't chop your father up like a chicken fricassee--he was right there, you know, Dr. Mandelbroit. He saw the whole thing, he has yortsayt after his father. No question, he says. Heart attack. He even tried to massage his chest, give him vi heyst unofficial--"

"Artificial--"

"Restoration, whatever. Anyway, he says it shouldn't be much of a problem. He'll be able to fix it."

My father would have wet himself laughing. He'd spent his whole life trying to be an ornament to the Torah, and all he'd managed to do was stick it in a pig-skin case. For the last six months, he and Dr. Mandelbroit had been shaking their fists at each other, and now here was the Doctor, risking the scorn of his colleagues and--who knows?--the loss of his professional reputation, for a prohibition he regarded as absolute bullshit. They'd reached an agreement at last; my father's shrouds were like a white flag, only the winner was holding it up.

They'd both spoken the words of the living God, but the halakha was always according to my father, and Dr. Mandelbroit could never forgive him for it. "Things are changing." He was on the phone as soon as he got to town; he organized a meeting to press "their" demands. "It's not Europe here, it isn't the depression, and the way the shul runs it's for"--they couldn't say greenhorns, not to their fathers--"It's for you, not for us. We want to sit with our wives, we want to know what's going on." Give them onions and garlic, caviar and shrimp salad. Give them "a rabbi, a *real* rabbi"--Danny Kaye in a car-coat, not an atavistic nightmare like my father--"With recognized qualifications, a college degree, and he shouldn't talk English like Mrs. Nussbaum."

At forty-one, my father was an old man, a strange visitor from another planet, graced with the power to make everything forbidden. And he really did talk English like Mrs. Nussbaum. But the pig lies in the mud, waving its cloven hooves in the air and cries, "Eat me, I'm kosher," while the foolish in Israel run for their forks: Benoit Mandelbroit, *Doctor* Benoit Mandelbroit, chief of psychiatry at The Saints Boris and Gleb Memorial Institute of Public Health, Benoit Mandelbroit spoke such a beautiful English you could die. He'd come from France sometime before the War, nobody seemed to know quite how or why, and he sounded like Menashe Skulnick playing Pepe le Moko. His father had been a rabbi--he was shipped back to Poland and died in a camp--but Dr. Mandelbroit was *Doctor* Mandelbroit; he believed in reason, progress and the unconscious, in the ineluctable rightness of his every simple utterance. Go ahead and ask him. He'd aim an explanatory boomerang of polysyllables just far enough over your head that he could watch it come back and stun him with his own acuity--and he carried a notebook for just such occasions. According to him, it was our human, not to mention our prophetically mandated Jewish duty to love everybody, even the Germans: it was only *history* and forces beyond their conscious control that turned them into fucking Krauts--and you weren't supposed to pay any attention when Lenny Nightingale started going around telling everybody that *history* and forces beyond his conscious control made him keep knocking up the waitresses in his nightclub. You weren't even supposed to *look* at Lenny's handpainted, glow-in-the-dark tie with the naked woman on it that said, "I was humiliated at Versailles."

No, according to Dr. Mandelbroit, real, supra-sexual love was the only answer: love your neighbour, love yourself, love all the antisemitn doubly hard--go ahead, *teach* em a lesson--be kind to your web-footed friends, but most of all love Dr. Benoit Mandelbroit, M.D., Ph.D., Friend of This and Fellow of That, whom the great and nameless Yiddish-speaking World-Spirit had sent all the way from France to this here Sinai of coulee-country to lead us out of the desert and into the twentieth century, world without end, hey bop a ree bop, amen, selah.

Us. A bunch of hunchbacked refugees from Pilsudski or the Czar who still kvelled and swooned over an active kid and called him a regular Babe Ruth; D.P.'s straight from the camps and D.P.'s like me and my family who'd somehow managed to miss them. We reeked of cholent, we looked like herring. We needed guidance.

It was the first election since 1924, when Khaim Mes flipped a coin with Khaim Jimmy Durante to see who got the shul and who the khevra kaddisha. Khaim Mes won, and Khaim Jimmy, my father's great-uncle who brought us over from Shanghai, became President for Life. Abie Doktor succeeded him in 1949, just twenty-four hours before the Uncle was to have claimed his golden kiddish cup, and he'd been acclaimed every year since. Architect of the Great Shift from shmaltz to milk herring at the weekday kiddish--two members were still on a food strike--he wasn't the sort of man to take crap from newcomers. "Im glist zikh azoy a big shot tsu zayn, He's got such a yen to be a big shot, Zul er dem koved farkrenkn, Let him spend the prestige on prescriptions." Abie Doktor abdicated, to be with the woman he loved. He went over the synagogue's books, translated them into Polish, and put the originals in his burner-barrel.

Fifteen minutes after he picked up the gavel, Dr. Mandelbroit was as lonely as a stone. Once his supporters discovered that even a reform rabbi with half a circumcision was going to cost a mansion more than cleaning fluid and kugel, they justified the way of the Tractates and turned Benoit into a janitor. With the exception of the female Mandelbroits, not a single person turned up for the round-table symposium on the moral meaning of the High Holidays but the alte Mrs. Reingewirtz, who wanted to take a nap before slikhes, the penitential prayers at midnight.

But Dr. Mandelbroit still had to show up at shul every Saturday and sit by the ark. The rest of his spare time was devoted to cleaning up the daily kiddish, ordering herring and dunning the members for their dues. He tried to step down right after Rosh Hashana, but Abie had started to bask in his golden years. He liked the peace and quiet; he enjoyed dropping a full plate at the kiddish every morning. He read brochures about Florida until well after Sukkes, measured Dr. Mandelbroit's weekly hair-loss, then finally called a meeting: "President for Life, and nothing less. And Shaye Levkes as executive assistant"--Abie was sick of mopping the floor and setting up chairs. He was seventy-eight years old and knew where the slivovitz was hidden. My father wanted to think it over--he'd been doing this stuff for years already, but Abie was one of ours--and Dr. Mandelbroit actually started to cry.

"You're still a fanatic, Shaye," Benoit brought over a bottle of Crown Royal to say thank you to my father, "But at least you aren't a hypocrite. If there's ever anything I can do for you..."

He didn't even wait to be asked. Dr. Mandelbroit had an eye for the underdeveloped, and he'd been seeing quite a lot of me lately; what with the opera records and artistic prints, the lectures on Freud's interpretation of shadkhn jokes, and the modern classics he gave me to read--The_World's Illusion, Thomas Mann, Jean-Christophe--I was starting to feel like Mrs. Reingewirtz waiting to repent.

Then came the biography of Leon Trotsky. "Leon Trotsky?" I said, as he shoved the book into my gut. "A sinner in Israel. A destroyer, a misleader and a bum." Dr. Mandelbroit gave me a look and motioned me to the dinner table. "I know," I said. "We have a friend who knew him before he was famous."

Dr. Mandelbroit was arching his brows like I'd told him that my orgasms were all clitoral. He leaned forward in his chair, stuck his elbows on the table and waved a forkful of steak under my nose. He knew I wouldn't eat in his house, so he made a

point of inviting me for supper every week to check for drool
and see if I'd crack. My mother would stuff me at home like it
was shabbes in Hollywood, and I'd bring along an apple, Dr.
Mandelbroit shouldn't think he was smart, to give me something
to do besides stare at Sabina. The Mandelbroits dined in
French--they did everything in French--and they never put the
chandail de mon oncle on the rez-de-chaussee--I couldn't
understand a word. I'd chomp and stare, envying every morsel
to penetrate Sabina's insides, until it was time to defend the
faith. Sabina and her sister had gone to Yiddish-language
secular schools before they came to Coalbanks, and Dr.
Mandelbroit seemed to feel that talking to me like I just got off
the boat was like some kind of vitamin for linguistic elan. He
wanted to know all about my family--how we got there, where
we spent the War, what it was like to be frum in Coalbanks--
pressing me for details about mikves and wigs, and winking at
his wife like I was an organ-grinder's monkey who thought he
was a boy, until I couldn't stand it anymore and told him that
even though I had payes and wore tsistis--I pulled them out of
my pants to show him--that didn't mean that I couldn't speak
English. I was even going to school, remember? But I must
have been too cute to leave alone.

"Leon Trotsky?" he chuckled. "You're sure you don't
mean Leon Brodsky?"

"Don't treat me like a fool, Dr. Mandelbroit. You know as
well as I do that Leon Brodsky owns a suit-shop on Tenth Street
and that knowing him isn't such a big achievement. When I say
Leon Trotsky," I exhaled an imaginary stream of cocktail-
cigarette smoke, "I mean Leon Trotsky."

Dr. Mandelbroit held up his empty fork. "All right. You
know then from Leon Trotsky. But which of your friends, or
your family's friends, is it who actually knew him?"

"Oh, a good friend of my father," I replied blithely. Dr.
Mandelbroit owned every book Kalman Franzoys had ever
published, and I wanted to hold off on the name as long as I
could. I wanted to see the look on his face when I showed him
that Kalman had even dedicated A Geshray fun Shangkhai, A Cry
from Shanghai, to my father.

"Knowing your father as I do, I find it hard to believe that
he has friends who would have known Leon Trotsky."

I shrugged my shoulders; it was my turn to smirk.

"What, one of your father's yeshiva-rebbes knew Trotsky even before the revolution?"

"He--the friend, not Trotsky--did used to learn with my father."

"What, the Dlugaszower Rebbe? That khnyok and Trotsky were maybe Mensheviks together? They should have made him commissar of gemore."

"Be reasonable, Doctor." Dr. Mandelbroit was always making fun of my father, and now was my chance to pay him back. I wanted him on his knees--to me, to my family, to everyone who still cared about the Torah.

"Well, then, tell me who it is." He sounded like a kid who wants an ice cream now.

"His name, you mean? Why didn't you say so in the first place?"

"Yes, yes. His name. Nu, zug shoyn. Tell me already."

"My father's friend, the one who doesn't know a Trotsky from a tallis?" Dr. Mandelbroit was nodding like a Slinky in heat. "Kalman Franzoys."

"Maleh vus a kind kon zugn, Go know what a kid'll say. Who the hell is Kalman Franzoys?" He was twisting around in his seat like the bathroom was closed for repairs.

"Oh, I'm sorry. I forgot." I'd learned the word ingenuous that summer, and I was beginning to like it. "That's just his nickname. On his books he's called Kalman Holzhacker."

Dr. Mandelbroit didn't say a word. His mouth dropped open and his eyes began to bulge like his brain was going to burst. He looked me up and down, could see that I wasn't lying--Kalman was virtually unknown in most religious households--and began to sputter all over my face.

I'd never seen him so excited about anything but himself. Ask him Diefenbaker, ask him Khruschev, ask him the etiology of the hangnail--Dr. Mandelbroit had the lowdown on everything, and unless you wanted the dew of his doctrine to drop all over your face--his teeth didn't quite line up, and he shpritsed whenever he was frantic--the best thing was to shut up and nod. Otherwise, he'd huk you a tshaynik, knock you a teapot, until you were blue in the face and wet as a fish. There was no yelling or screaming--that was beneath him; you had to be convinced, and with every reason in the book. He'd drone on and on, with only the pitter-patter of sputum on your cheeks to keep you conscious, reeling away in a flat, dispassionate Yiddish so full of two dollar words you were afraid he was going to ask for change.

He sounded about as Jewish as Arthur Godfrey. Not that there was anything *wrong* with his Yiddish--I'd heard enough bad Yiddish to last me a lifetime--but until I heard Benoit Mandelbroit in full flight, God help me, I'd never heard Protestant Yiddish. Even-handed, other-cheeked, big-hearted in its rush to victory. Never a curse and rarely a wish. Not even his bitterest enemy, not even my father or Abie Doktor, ever grew like an onion with his head in the ground or hung a lung and liver on the Doctor's nose. He sounded like a Yiddish insurance policy, but he didn't cover rain.

"Kalman Holzhacker!" A gentle spray, like the rebound from a dentist's water-drill, was dappling my face. "Your father knows Kalman Holzhacker?" I could see the dawn of a new esteem. "A sage, a genius, one of the most important writers of the century. If he wrote in anything but Yiddish, *anything*, he'd be world-famous by now." He slammed his fist onto the table like he was chairing a meeting. "Regardless of my daughters' tittering."

He should have known better. Genia and Sabina had been biting their lips and avoiding each other's eyes since I mentioned Leon Trotsky, bubbling and seething and writhing in their seats to preserve the fifth commandment; their father might have laughed at religion, but nobody laughed at their father. And they'd stopped laughing at anything already, they were giggling at their own giggles, when Dr. Mandelbroit had to slip into English and say "tittering"--like Genia could ever have drowned. She started snorting like a wild boar and coughed a blast of half-chewed something onto the front of Sabina's white blouse. Sabina looked, her mother squealed; Sabina licked a finger and rubbed it in good. The Dr. and Mrs. were gaping with professional dismay; a string of brownish retardo-spit was unreeling through a cleft in Genia's make-up, meandering along her chin like water in an irrigation ditch, getting longer, more bottom-heavy, until it finally plopped onto her sweatshirt.

It was all my fault. We'd been farting around in Dr.

Mandelbroit's study one day, looking for pictures of precocious puberty and advanced V.D., when I spotted a complete set of Kalman's poetry on one of the shelves. "A friend of the family," I said, winking to Sabina. "He taught me everything I used to know about women." Naturally, they didn't believe me, so I explained all about my parents and Kalman and Shanghai; I told them about Paris and his famous friends, about the Dlugaszower Rebbe and Kalman's rabbinic ordination, finishing up with *Nudist Life* and Kalman's visit--"My father threw him out the day before I met you"--and how he claimed that his smut was good for the Jews, as long as they didn't look at it. I showed them the dedication to the Shanghai book and the poems about my father in it.

By the end of the afternoon we had ourselves a secret human decoder ring and teenage pervert idol who made Elvis Presley look like Albert Schweitzer. Kalman was perfect-- anything that touched him turned into a joke, especially if you weren't alone. And we didn't need any handshakes or stupid hats, either; we had the Word, the Manual, the Talmud Franzoys, and all it cost us was a trip to Shmiley's and two bucks over the cover price: *Stars in Garters: Bouncing Babes of Burlesk Bare All*--and no naturist foreskins to worry about.

These were the broads that the ones in *Nudist Life* used to clean for, and if most of them were a little bald around the middle...Genia said that real artist's models, who were all lady bohemians *par excellence*, shaved their crotches for artistic reasons, but she only slapped her head and sighed when I aked her what they were. It was no big deal, anyway; a trainload of saltpetre couldn't have stopped these pictures, and not even Rahab in her splendour could have come close to the descriptions. Forget about pubic hair, this stuff was such Art it made *Nudist Life* read like *Dog of Flanders*. All the girls had Hebrew or Yiddish names; not names, exactly, but Hebrew and Yiddish phrases that Kalman had turned into names: Dina de Malchusa, the belly dancer, whose name meant law of the land; a sister act, Tess and Tisha Buvv, two ways of saying the Ninth of Av, the day the Temple was destroyed; an East Indian called Kashmir Intukas on a stuffed tiger; and five or six others. Sabina and I damn near laughed our lunch up once we finally noticed the commentary--Kalman had exceeded even *my* expectations--but

Genia fell prey to *poete maudit*, dropping real tears onto cabaret cutie Esther Tannis like this was *Lust for Life* in ladies' foundations. "Every picture, every paragraph, must be a knife in his heart." It didn't matter that his poetry was beyond her--the Yiddish was way too hard, even with my explanations--she could sense his greatness, and his torment.

She was the artistic type, Genia, as full of shit as a pigeon on Pesakh and just as down to earth--always carrying on about man's inhumanity to man and telling you how shallow you were. She was already fifteen, she'd spent her life in Alberta and slept with a night-light, but Genia was dying for espresso. She was an existentialist, a daughter of the Left Bank, a Juliette Greco in training addicted to her parents' *Paris Match* magazines. She wore nothing but black. Her hair was black, too, as limp and stringy as month-old coleslaw, and she paved her face with some kind of white cement that used to crack whenever she talked, and made her skin break out like a strawberry patch. A farzeyenish, my mother used to call her, a monster, such a freak of nature that nobody but me and Shmiley ever seemed to notice that she had a build out of Kalman's pin-ups: perfect, tapering legs and a set of knockers that were the bane of her existence. Pictures of Audrey Hepburn and Leslie Caron in the frame of Genia's mirror didn't change a thing; her body weight was still half tits, no matter what she did to hide them. She wore oversize sweaters twelve months a year, and hunched herself over like she was passing a stone. She was never not reading *Bonjour Tristesse*.

She flipped for Kalman, filling her diary with confidential love-notes that she recited from the top of the basement stairs while Sabina and I tickled each other and tried not to laugh. "Giggle, Philistines": freed from his soul-destroying slavery and redeemed by Genia's love, Kalman would go on to his crowning achievement, embracing Genia twenty-four hours a day while she, a great believer in her thesaurus, wallowed in his mature good looks and the fineness of his perceptions; with Genia's help and inspiration, he'd endite the greatest Yiddish poem of all times and places.

"With one hand?" Sabina yelled up. "What's he gonna call it, *Genia Gives*?" Genia tried to barricade us downstairs with a coffee table; she broke two of her mother's Wedgwood ashtrays and scraped half the flesh from her shin.

She was so far gone, she started writing poetry herself, then asked me to translate it into Yiddish. "I need to speak in the language of his heart."

"Better you should send him a kugel." For the first time in my life, I really felt like the old men I was always imitating. "Yiddish, yet?" I shrugged and gave a wave with my hand. "Ekh mir a language of love."

Genia called me insensitive. I got hold of a picture of Kalman, tubby and unshaven, and did my imitations again, but no one short of Kalman himself could convince her that his heart's only language was a lip-fart.

Dr. Mandelbroit to the contrary, Kalman was about as famous as anyone who writes poems about Jews can get. He'd been translated into twenty-seven languages, and professors from India to Ethiopia, from coast to coast, goyim who felt bad about World War II, kept sending him letters--"For toilet paper, I gotta pay," he wrote my father--begging him to explain some of his jewier allusions--"And it don't even lick": especially those to that mythological figure or folklore hero or pagan idol in Jewish disguise, the Shaye Levkes that he kept invoking in *A Geshray fun Shangkhai.*

It took a genius like Peter Paul Schimmelweiser, Adjunct Professor of Prophecy at the Casper Scripture Academy, Casper, Wyoming, to solve the riddle. Professor Schimmelweiser had figured out that Yishayohu Levkes, the full Hebrew form of the name, could be rearranged to spell ilui-oysek-yeshue, a prodigy busy with the redemption, thus providing final and definitive proof that the search for a real-life Levkes prototype must perforce begin and end with Jesus, Yeshue, of Nazareth, the very prodigy of redemption himself. The professor was likewise heartened to have gleaned--from the German translation of the poems--that Kalman's privations in the Shanghai ghetto had opened his eyes to the truth that would set him free, and he signed his letter, "Your brother in Christ."

My father was so taken with being Jesus, that he forgave Kalman immediately. "Nu, Rukhl," he read the letter out loud at supper-time, "Ja sadze, Polsku Polish."

"Phnyeh," said my mother. "Kalman do Madagaskaru, let him go to Madagascar." It's what the Polish khamehs used to yell about the Jews.

"Yeah, but think of the boy. If I'm the Yoizele--"

"Ligt *er* in drerd un bakt beygl, he's up shit creek, baking bagels."

"Un s'vet im helfn vi der farayuriker shnay, it'll help him like the neiges d'antan."

And Kalman didn't stop with my father; he also enclosed a copy of his letter to the professor, congratulating him on being "the first and only man fully to understand both me and my work," and requesting a small donation to further Christ's cause among the Jews.

I wiped the calf's foot jelly from the letter and dried it on my night-table lamp. The way Genia blushed and cried and started acting almost normal, you'd have thought she was having Kalman's baby. She even insisted on coming down to the basement with me and Sabina to star in our new, Kalman-based sex-game, and she threw herself into it with all the fervour of a penitent. Wearing one of her father's old shirts with no bra underneath, bending and stretching while I pretended to snap her picture--this was like eating on Yom Kippur for her--she finally slipped to the floor...in a languid sprawl. Her panties must have been left over from kindergarten--you could practically see what Shmiley used to call "the whole organ"--and we named her Charna Peltz, Black Fur-Coat, after the line of hair that ran south from her pipik like a widening river. Our fake descriptions were even more fun than the posing, and we made her into a hot-blooded Eskimo pie: "Just ask the men who moyel for gold."

Dr. Mandelbroit gave me the Trotsky book two days later, and it was 'nuff said for the girls as soon as I mentioned our friend. Sabina finally managed to explain that it was the name that struck them funny--Holzhacker means woodcutter in Yiddish, and isn't always quite as neutral as Sawyer. The girls' grasp of the nuances of mama-loshn so stirred Dr. Mandelbroit's fatherly pride--"You've been a good influence, Yoinele"--that he bought the whole thing, and excused the girls to go wipe themselves off.

We were alone now. Mrs. Mandelbroit knew what was coming and fled with the girls, while her husband charged forward like nothing had happened. "Genius?" he asked rhetorically. According to him, Kalman Franzoys was the only man alive, with the possible exception of Benoit Mandelbroit- -who was, don't forget, the son of a rabbi--who really understood the nature of Judaism; as if the rest of us had converted or something. He was also a saint of the Yiddish word; ravens brought him money, it rained down like manna from heaven with a bonus every Friday, while Kalman sat and sifted iambs from morning to night--and I had to sit there like a lawn-chair, creaking under his asshole gravity and never giving up a groan. Go tell him that his hero peddled smut--Dr. Mandelbroit was a grown-up, a family man; he was Sabina's father and could cause me plenty of grief. Tell him the truth about Kalman, you might as well tell an interfaith shaygets that religious Jews wave live chickens around their heads on the eve of Yom Kippur-- even if you're proud of it, you're still an antisemit, which in Dr. Mandelbroit's books was an Enemy of Art. He would have thrown me out of the house.

Of course, things weren't much better when Sabina came by us. Friday night, before the big weekly make-out session, my father and I would return from shul to find Sabina and my mother waiting for us, their faces as shabbesdik and smooth as a couple of brand new bowling balls. We'd sing *Sholem Aleikhem* and "A woman of valour"--I used to try and wink at Sabina-- then make kiddish and sit down to eat, while my parents tried to figure out what kind of a home Sabina came from.

"Would you say," the first words my father ever spoke to her, the soup dribbling off his spoon and back into the bowl,

"That existence," the *very* first words, after a cursory nod and grunt in her direction,

"Precedes essence," he'd known she was coming, knew who she was and who was her father;

"Or that a man, a human being," she was Jewish, she was pretty, she was dangerous as hell,

"Is such in all essentials before he's even in the womb?"

I wanted to die. "Shabbes, tatte," I cried. "Host shoyn fargesen in western hospitality?" Sabina couldn't understand this kind of Yiddish, and my translations were as helpful as

Pope Pius. She'd hem and haw--my father was waiting for an answer--kick me gently under the table and finally come out with something that could see the merit in both sides of the argument.

"Aha!" My father's finger would rise like Moses' staff. "So if we know that a human being is not going to give birth to a cat or a dog or God forbid a bunny rabbit, then the essence must be somehow determined before that human being's even been conceived in its mother's womb. No?" My father's notions of modern thought came from Hitler and the Yiddish press, and from Hitler we didn't talk on shabbes. "So, if the essence of a human being is determined long before he--*or she*," he'd add, looking Sabina straight in the eye, "Sees the light of day, then it stands to reason that there must be some power--mind you, I'm not saying what or where"--*The Magic Mountain* was starting to look good to me--"There must be some power that determines the various and sundry natures of species and individuals alike, and this power must be both prior to and outside of the processes which it sets into being. Yoinele, translate."

He was into the gefilte fish. "And if such a power were to issue a set of rules for the regulation of human life, would you not feel it incumbent upon you to follow such a code?" He'd sweep his fish through the khreyn and conclude in triumph. "What can Dr. Mandelfreud say to that?"

Sabina never had any answer; she was too busy trying to chew her matseballs. And now my father's eternal comfort depended entirely on Benoit Mandelbroit, who couldn't lose as long as he tried. Even if they threw him out of the hospital and julienned my father so that he'd go to greet the Messiah wearing an olive slice for a yarmulke, it wouldn't be because Benoit Mandelbroit hadn't done his best.

"*Now* you look human again." I opened my eyes as soon as the rubbing stopped and found myself staring straight into the face of Florence Gurfein, mother of Stevie, the Red Menace. "What the hell happened to you, anyway?" "Shock?" I asked her. Why start up? She patted me on the shoulder. I figured her cleaning me up sort of balanced-out Stevie's snowballs.

"Shock," she repeated. "Poor thing." She smiled without opening her mouth and started stroking my yarmulke like it was a lucky hunchback. The rest of the women were fixing coffee or clucking their tongues, some natives in the living room were groaning over Perry Como, and Khaim was signaling his return with a ritual knocking on the open apartment door, using Stevie Gurfein's head for knuckles.

Religion had nothing to do with it. Professional wrestling was the magnificent obsession of every older Jewish male, regardless of synagogue attendance or ritual observance, and Khaim had been loading his own furniture truck for years. He had the kid in a headlock, his favourite hold, and was crowning every slam with another curse: "Pig-dick, Nazi, afterbirth. The gallows are too good for such a"--he had to stop to think of a word--"For such a bloody little PISSFUCK!"--I thought Stevie's head was going to break open--"Like you are."

"Murderer!" Mrs. Gurfein let go of my head and started towards Khaim.

"C'mon and take him." It was statement of fact, not a challenge. "You'll wanna give him, too." He'd let off banging Stevie's head, and the jerk lay slumped in his arms, pimples all inflamed. You could almost hear the tweeting birds.

"The orphan"--Khaim held up a hand and gestured at me--"Did he come home like an orphan, or like the scene of an accident? Nu?"

"He looked like hell," said Mrs. Gurfein. "But he said that his nose started bleeding when he--when he heard."

"A tsaddik." Khaim beamed at me. "It started bleeding when he heard. And the Mormon Tabernacle Choir, that's what he heard?" He gave a mock chuckle. "Sam Levenson!"--Stevie's head hit the door and Mrs. Gurfein winced--"Sam Levenson and Jack Benny, Jr., *that's* what he heard, laughing and throwing snowballs at the orphan and me. And not just any snowballs, either. C'mon, Parkyerkarkass"--whonk!--"Tell em how funny you made it. Tell em what was *in* the snowballs."

"Rocks." Khaim had shifted him to a half-nelson, and Stevie was looking at the floor. "We put rocks in the snowballs."

His mother walked up and slapped Stevie across the face.

"Nu, what'd I tell you?" asked Khaim contentedly.

"You put what in where?!" Mrs. Gurfein hit Stevie again. "Nu, I'm waiting."

"We put rocks in the snowballs."

Again across the face. "I'll put a rock in *your* snowball." Stevie cringed, tried to duck, but she didn't hit him; she wanted to know who was we.

Stevie shook his head. "Tough guy, huh? Code of the gangster, eh, you mamzer?" She gave him another swat. "Yoine!" she turned to me. "Who was it?"

I grinned. "Ask Stevie," I said.

"Nu?" He was crying by now, begging me for mercy with his eyes. If they heard about this at school, he'd end up in another toilet. "You gonna tell me, or--"

Serel Efsherke came ploughing her way through the crowd, a twelve-inch kitchen knife in her hand. "Here." She handed it to Mrs. Gurfein. "This they always understand."

"NU?" Mrs. Gurfein shoved the blade into the doorjamb, and Stevie's pimples turned white. "Now tell me who was with you."

"Bruce Wohlgelernter." He sounded like a door in a horror movie.

His mother recoiled like from a side of pork. "The Tumour?" A buzz went up from the crowd. "And it was his idea to attack Joey and Mr. Shpilkover like that? Tell me the truth."

"Not really."

"Not really? So it was your idea then?"

"I guess so."

Mrs. Gurfein turned to the crowd. "He guesses." She took a look at the knife, pulled it loose and slapped him on the thigh with the blunt side. "I'll give you *three* guesses, you hoodlum, you! You think it's funny to attack an orphan and an old man in broad daylight, I'll give you a laugh you'll never forget."

"We didn't know he was an orphan." His batteries were just about dead.

"And if Mr. Levkes hadn't passed away this morning, it would have been all right?" The rest of the women were nodding. Mrs. Gurfein wasn't very religious, but no one could deny that she had a Jewish heart. "And tell me, Jesse Owens, how is it that you're here and The Tumour isn't?"

Stevie had no chance to answer. Khaim pointed at me and drew a finger across his throat, then looked at Mrs. Gurfein with rueful sympathy. "My Dovidl, nebekh, he at least doesn't know what he's doing--and even he would never commit such a crime. But your son..Blimeh"--that's Florence in Yiddish; Khaim had known her since she was a kid--"All I got to say is, when the hand speaks, the tukhes pays attention. You khap?"

"*He'll* khap," said Mrs. Gurfein menacingly. "Won't you, Stevie? I'll tear the pimples right off your face." He could have thrown the same snowball yesterday and no one would have noticed but me. But Mrs. Gurfein still wasn't finished. "I'll--I'll--Ohp, the girlfriend." She stepped out of the doorway and in walked Sabina, her pancake streaked with tears, a kerchief on her head like we were still in Poland.

We couldn't hug and kiss like human beings, not in front of all these parents, so we took each other's hand and everything else disappeared. It was Sabina, after all, more beautiful to me than ever; her anguished pout and perfect tears, the mucous coating her braces--*now* it came out of me, all the crying I'd been too busy to bother about, just like I was finally alone. "Joey," she said, and buried her head in my shoulder.

I didn't know where to put my other hand. Where it should have gone--shit, they'd have thought it was cute, so I settled for stroking the back of her neck, giving a little pinch of a squeeze so she'd know how I wanted to hug her. "Copine." I'd learned it from her. "How come you're not at school?"

She sort of wiped her nose on the arm-loop of my tsitses--nobody'd remembered to bring me a shirt--looked at my freshly cleaned face and started blubbering even harder.

"Nu, Yoinele." Khaim was calling me back to reality. "You want I should give him again?"

"Luz shoyn oop." The faster they finished with Stevie, the sooner Sabina and I could go to my room. "Leave it be." Khaim shrugged and let him go.

Sabina licked my shoulder and squeezed my hand. "You see," somebody said behind us, "A real tsaddik, just like the father." My voice had stayed level through the tears , and they must have confused it with the scales of justice. Mrs. Gurfein turned around and came piously to my side. She put her hand on my empty shoulder like she thought she was reading my mind, then reached her arm right around me and undid Sabina's kerchief with a single pluck at her chin. "Poor dears," she said. "You get so mad sometimes, you forget there's people with real tsuris."

What they didn't know, wouldn't hurt them--I was also afraid of birds. Mrs. Gurfein and the rest of the ladies were so lost in veneration that they would have turned me into an Italian screen-door, if my mother hadn't floated into the kitchen, happy as the dope-fiends in our health-class movies. "Does my boy need his mother?" At least her hair was covered. "Maybe you forgot your lunch?"

It must have been elephant tranquilizers that Dr. Mandelbroit sent over. If I was going to hold her and kiss her and cry all over her like I was doing to Sabina--and let her do the same to me in front of all these people--I only wanted she should know how come. She knew that my father was dead the way I knew it was Christmas Eve. Otherwise, she wouldn't have been humming. "Nu, Mama, go back to bed, why don't you? You've gotta be ready, you know." I still wouldn't say what for.

But my mother had ideas of her own. "Ready? 'Kh bin shoyn ready. I sewed myself shrouds while we were still in Shanghai. Just give me five minutes to change--nu, Serel, you better take me to the mikve first--and I'll be ready to get in there with him. Oy, Shaye, shvants vus di bist"--asshole?--"Host indz farluzn af hefker, You've thrown us up for scrambles."

Mrs. Gurfein squeezed one of my shoulders, Sabina was biting the other, I was almost happy to be so stupid, and Serel Efsherke--she might have been a bitch, but she never lost her head--had her lips around my ear, telling me what to say. "Bist aroop fin zinen?" I felt like Velvel, the Jewish dummy on the TV; if I'd been made of wood, my face would have warped. "You out of your mind? We'd have to bury you on the railway tracks."

My mother looked at me and burst into tears. "G'rutn in tatn," she was hiccupping. "The image of his father, like two drops of water." It was Serel who had named her Rukhl-Mayn-Heiliker-Tatte, and she knew damned well that my mother'd rather listen to the dead. "Gey shlufn, mama." It was my one original thought. "Nothing'll get any worse."

Twice in five minutes, give a look on a prophet. "It came early this year, Neville Chamberlain's birthday?" Mrs. Wohlgelernter had the patience of the Angel of Death coming back for his keys. She put her hands on her hips and shoved through to my mother like the rest of the room was empty; her left elbow caught Stevie square in the gut. "A gantser yontef do," she reached for my mother's collar and ended up with Serel's forearm, "A regular holiday here, and *my* son's gonna spend *his* holidays, God knows the rest of his life, in the hospital."

"It could always be worse." I recognized Shifra Dropdead's accent. To the Tumour's mother, we were all a bunch of pre-toilet paper D.P.'s, so whenever she spoke to us in Yiddish--if that's what you wanted to call it--we made a point of answering her in English.

"It could be worse?" she asked Shifra. "It should be worse for you, you Galitsyaner garbage." Shifra had spent four years in Mauthausen. Her husband ran away in 1951, and she once lost a baby 'cause he kicked her in the stomach. Nobody really like Shifra, but even Sabina, who hardly even knew her, straightened up and wiped her nose.

Mrs. Wohlgelernter didn't notice. "Forget everything else, I just want you should know, *Rebbetsin*, that your religious boy hot my son a kick geton in"--she didn't know a polite Yiddish word--"In di testicles arayn, he came home vomiting and he still hasn't stopped." I could hear Stevie sighing.

My mother said testicles, sort of, and started to laugh; she had no idea what it meant. Serel was standing in front of her now, gazing at Mrs. Wohlgelernter with all the tenderness of a fly-swatter, while my mother planned her future in a normal tone of voice: Should she join my father in her hair, her kerchief or her wig, and should it be the weekday or the shabbes wig.

"You stupid fucking cunt." The Efsherke's English was just as good as her Yiddish. "Testicles should grow out of your liver."

She looked, Mrs. Wohlgelernter, like Hitler'd stuck his finger in her chewing gum; there was foam pouring over her lips. Florence Gurfein ran over and started lecturing in a whisper, pointing to Stevie and explaining the whole thing. Sylvia hadn't even known that my father was dead. She apologized to my mother, who wished her a good testicles, and finally declared, "Sometimes I think the doctors were right." Nobody contradicted her, and she stole out of the apartment like her falsies had burst.

"Yoinele." My mother started talking as soon as Sylvia left. "Ikh bin tshikaveh tsu visn, I'm curious to know, Vi azoy hobn oysgezen by Brucie di tentsicles?"

What did they look like? I almost broke down completely; she thought the kick had been in Yiddish--a look, I mean. Even Shifra Dropdead, who thought vagina was in Saskatchewan, was rolling her eyes.

Serel clapped her hand over my mother's mouth and got her out of there before she said anything else. My longed-for hour had come at last. Mrs. Gurfein sent Stevie back to school and Khaim went to meet the khevra kaddisha. They'd forgotten all about me, so Sabina and I went off to my room. I had to put on a shirt.

"How'd you get here?" I asked, after we'd finished hugging and kissing and crying some more. "And how'd you know what happened?"

"The whole school knows, darling." I was sure that Khaim had been speaking Yiddish. "And Shmiley can't understand?" He even tried to get the rehearsal called on account of respect, but Mr. Dee just grabbed his bleeding nose and said, "The show must go on," before giving my part to somebody else.

"But how'd you get outta school?"

"I barfed on Colleen Semple." I was so proud of her, the real and true 4-ever love of my life. Not only could Sabina belch to order better than any guy I ever knew--and I'm talking about the national sport of Coalbanks here--she could also throw up whenever she wanted. And on Colleen Semple, yet, that buck-toothed scrag with the glasses whose mother was women's editor at *The Coalbanks Frontiersman*. The whole town knew too much about Colleen already, but *we* had to fucking live with her: she was a born teacher, a sensible teen, a regular church-goer who liked Liberace. Not even hoods like Greg Ramsay thought she needed a good fuck. And to think that Sabina, who sat behind her, had fulfilled the whole class's dream, and that I was the inspiration--I had to kiss her all over again.

I wanted to go farther, my hands were crying out for her blouse. I wanted to hold her like I should have been holding my mother--the jerks who called Sabina "fried eggs" didn't know what they were missing--but it wouldn't've been right, not then, and she knew it, too. So we stayed ankle to ankle, twisting to each other at the edge of the bed, my knuckles on Sabina's knees while I held onto both of her hands.

She was too smart to ask me any questions, and I didn't have the faintest idea. As far as I could figure, my mother'd take over the store and I'd go back to school. Nothing would change, except my father wouldn't be there.

Of course, there'd be no more gemore lessons every day, no Hebrew books left around for me to read. Nobody'd tell me stories about yeshivas in the old country or sneaking into the movies in Poland when religious boys weren't supposed to go, but my father was so in love with Tom Mix and his horse Tony--I never found out if they called him Antek in Polish--that he was willing to risk the wrath of his parents and a fight with the Jewish goyim who hung around the kino, just for a chance to see him. And how when the War was over and he managed to locate his great-uncle Khaim, whom he'd never met--that's Khaim Jimmy Durante, because people used to stop him on the street for autographs and Khaim always obliged, signing Khaim ben Alexander Zishe in Hebrew and then giving out with an accented ha-cha-cha--when he found Khaim, or maybe Khaim found us, I was never quite sure, and discovered that his religious uncle was leading a religious life in the middle of the western plains--sure, he wanted to be with family, but that was the real clincher. I couldn't remember it--my father had to tell me something else he'd never tell me again--how Khaim showed up at the train station in a big white cowboy hat, carrying three more, S, M and L, one inside the other like a peddler back home, and stuck them on us as we came off the platform, laughing and crying and hugging these people he'd never seen before, shouting "Brukhim ha-bu'im in Kanade, welcome to Canada, udim mutsalim, brands rescued from the fire, ha-cha-cha"; and made my father go to shul the next morning and bentsh goymel, say the prayer of deliverance, while wearing his white cowboy hat. And I was right beside him the whole time, all of maybe three years old, the hat somewhere over my nose, asking my father where all the soldiers were.

"I've still got it," I told Sabina, and I went and took the hat out of my closet.

"You shoulda been with me in the cowgirls," she said. "You'd make a cute little girl." I scowled. "But I like you better as a man." Another reason I loved her--she was the first person in the world ever to call me a man, and she really thought I was. A grown-up, capable, real man--a little light on the facial hair--the way every thirteen year old sees himself.

"And did I tell you how my father and mother met when they were like refugees in Vilna?" A hundred times. "And how a Russian wanted like a *favour* from my mother, so my father ran up and told him to watch out, the bitch already gave *him* a disease, so the Russian gave him cigarettes? Did I tell you?" A thousand times, but she heard it out again and again, until we'd probably relived my parents' whole lives there on my bed. She was like being alone with myself, only without the recriminations.

"But what about your mother, Joey? You think she'll get married again?"

"Never." There was no question. We sat there for a minute or two. "Who could she marry in a place like this?"

"But I thought--aren't you supposed to get married again inside of a year?"

"Maybe in New York you are, but not here."

"And if they arranged something, sent somebody out here?"

"I'd kick his ass." Don't ask me how it slipped out, but I meant it, anyway.

"I'm sorry, Joey."

"Oy, Sabina"--you could tell where I'd learned my love-talk--"What are we gonna do?"

We stared at each other for the next two hours. I cried, Sabina cried, we stared at the floor and cried together. I tried to explain to her that I wouldn't be able to go to the movies or listen to music for the next eleven months, but she already knew all about it. "It doesn't matter, Joey," she told me, then added with a Yiddish smile, "Abi mit dir tsu zayn, As long as I can be with you." It's a line from a folksong.

The Efsherke klapped on the door to tell us that Sabina's father had turned up, and that we'd better be behaving ourselves in there. I threw on a shirt, Sabina too--I'd fallen so far as to rest my head on her brassiere--and we went out to see the Doctor.

"It cost me," he said immediately in Yiddish, "But I did it. You don't have to thank me, Yoine. Your father and I might have disagreed about everything under the sun, but we respected each other's opinion." I was in no condition to tell him the truth. "It's the least I could do. We were the only intellectuals in this...excuse for a town...Not to mention the, uh, family connections." He switched straight into French, but all I could catch was ecole. Sabina threw in an amour.

"Nu, Dr. Mandelbroit." Shifra Dropdead was dying to know. "Zug shoyn, tell us already."

"Borukh-a-shem," he said. If this didn't bring my father back, nothing would. "Like I told the boy, it cost me--don't worry about it--but Shaye Levkes is as intact as the Matke Boske, the Mother of God, and the remains are already with the khevra kaddisha. You've been very lucky, Yoinele, you and your entire family."

Sabina took my hand; they say in Yiddish that a putz makes children, and Sabina knew it, too. "What about my mother?" I asked. "She's walking around like one of your patients."

Dr. Mandelbroit nodded and looked at his watch. "She should be all right by now. She's sleeping?" Serel blessed God. "Good. Best thing for her. Khaim phoned me at the shul after he ran back here with the news, said she wouldn't stop screaming, not even to take a breath. So loud, he said, that the Mrs. from next door--"

"Mrs. Jurychuk--"

"Azoy, ran in without even knocking. She thought there'd been a murder. So I sent over some tranquilizers, nothing worse should befall her."

"But she doesn't even know where she is!" I hollered. "And she wants to throw herself into the grave!"

"She'll be ok when she wakes up."

"Normal, you mean?"

"As normal as possible, under the circumstances."

"Nu then, zug mir, Dr., you're a physician. Why? How is it that such a thing can happen?"

Dr. Mandelbroit shrugged his shoulders. He'd never not known anything before. "It happens," was all he could say.

I was crying again, Sabina too, even the doctor was rubbing his eyes. "I'm so proud of you, Papa," Sabina said in French. "You've done so much, and none of it for you."

Dr. Mandelbroit shrugged her off. "Yoinele," he said, "It's probably too soon to tell you, but I just want you to know--I know that nothing can replace your father, not for you and not for us, but if you should ever need help or...or fatherly advice, please don't be ashamed to come to me. In view of our...family circumstances"--he made a semi-circle with each hand, like he was blessing his flock--"I already feel like something of a father to you. And you know," and he started blinking at his shoes, as if he'd seen some birdshit shoot down, "If my daughter can feel for you as much as she does, how can I not love you, too?"

It was like hearing that my Latin exam was the cure for cancer. If Dr. Mandelbroit could love me, could admit it in public, in Yiddish, in front of a roomful of people who couldn't get excited in anything else--forget the meshiekh, Jesus was probably coming. And it never rains but it pours; he came over and embraced me. And stroked my head. And said, "Forget the doctor, we don't need to be so formal. You can call me Ben-Tsiyon."

Ben-Tsiyon, Benye, Bentse--my father drops dead and all of a sudden I'm on a first-name basis with the head of the khevra kaddisha and the biggest--maybe the only--psychiatrist in town. "Ben-Tsiyon." There wasn't much else to say. "Well, please continue to call me Yoine."

Dr. Mandelbroit, Ben-Tsiyon, chuckled his way out of the embrace and went back to check on my mother, taking Serel along as chaperone. The phone rang--it had been ringing all morning--Mrs. Gurfein listened for a minute, then sent Sabina to get her father. "He had to call collect yet," she spat into a kleenex, "And ask for Mr. Levkes."

Dr. Mandelbroit looked annoyed. He picked up the phone in English, then switched abruptly into Jewish. "Rabbi Applebaum? What are you doing in Vulcan?" He hmmed and mmed some, came out with two leaping "what"'s, scratched his head, furrowed his brow, stroked his goatee and hung up in disgust. He dialed someone right away. "Khaim?" he yelled into the phone; he laid the receiver on his shoulder for almost half a minute. "Wait 'til you hear before you start cursing. It's the tanna, the mishnaic sage, from Calgary...Of course, he won't be here; he slid off the road just outside Vulcan, hit epes an ice patch and messed up the car, it wouldn't be ready before tomorrow if tomorrow wasn't Christmas...What? I don't know what, I only know what he told me, 'farkrimt epes a wheel'. Probably threw them out of alignment when he hit the sign...Don't be silly, his wife's as blind as Isaac...What else? I'll tell you what else. The shlimazl opens the door, he slips on the same ice--for rubbers he's too elegant, the Beau Brummel--and sprains himself an ankle...Don't look at me, Khaim, I didn't ordain him. So he's stuck in Vulcan"--about fifty miles north of Coalbanks--"He's got a bandage on his foot and a cane in his hand, his car's as crippled as he is and," Dr. Mandelbroit started laughing, "And he's wondering where he'll eat...Take it easy, Khaim, I'll go up and get him, but we'll never be ready before sundown--he wants me to find him a specialist...Don't worry, I'll tell him. And I'll tell him who said it." Dr. Mandelbroit laughed, sighed, put down the phone and reached for his keys--then he remembered my mother. "The putz, I'll give him what to eat." He looked at me and turned his palms to the ceiling. "I'm sorry, Yoine. It'll have to be tomorrow," and then headed back to the bedroom.

Tomorrow? Trust Rabbi Applebaum. He used to shake with his hands at the best of times, the moyel. Tomorrow? Shit. What was I supposed to do until tomorrow? Already the ladies were getting ready to leave--the big shock, the big rush was all over now--and pretty soon I'd be left alone with my mother. You could smell my father's cigarettes, his gemore was sitting on the coffee table. What were we going to talk about when she finally came to? Sabina was squeezing my hand, and I still felt all alone. "I think I need a nap," I said. I was hoping I'd never wake up. Sabina followed me back to the bedroom and took a book from her purse. I gave her the bed and curled up on the floor. I dreamt that my father had died.

III

From the time the goysess waves good-bye with his soul until some Christmas observing business acquaintance dumps the final shovel of earth on the coffin, you can feel what you feel and think what you think--you're only a shade to the Jews. Funeral business aside--making arrangements, conveying the news--no one's allowed to talk to you first; you should go to them, and all they're going to say is "I'm sorry." You're like Scrooge with the ghosts, only Cratchit repents.

You can't sit on a chair or sleep in a bed. A low stool by day, at night there's the floor. But don't worry--Mr. Sandman can't talk to you, either. You can lie on the floor, toss and turn on spruce, fir, pine, go to sleep in your balsa wood airplane or cuddle up with Mortimer Snerd. You can wake up, I mean stand up, I mean drag your calloused ass aloft with a mouth full of dust and ashes from a gantse nakht breathing rug.

Or you can sit up all night and hope the shoymer, the bodyguard, is as wakeful as you are; you can imagine the rats on the body if Khaim should doze off. You can pace and grumble, rend your heart and tear your hair, talk to your Maker or talk to the wall--the choice is yours, the wall you can hit.

So I sat on the floor and talked to myself. I wanted to weep like a kidnapped Cossack, wipe my nose and say I'd done no wrong, but God would have laughed in my face: *God* made my father happy, *I* was the one who killed him. I was Man the fucking Maker--too short to strangle him, I couldn't find a knife, my mother would have heard the gunshots, so I turned myself into a tool, a finely-tuned instrument that didn't know what it was doing. I went to scratch my name on a flint-tipped chisel and burned down the whole fucking village. I'd been culpable, treacherous, thieving; I'd snuck Presley records into the house and was up to three cigarettes a day; I'd read nudist books--in a room full of gemores, yet--and dishonoured Sabina Mandelbroit with up to three fingers at a time; I'd spilled my seed to waste all over the place, more often, I was sure, than my parents had ever had sex, and I'd eaten a french fry--once, for the thrill; I puked. I'd shot my mouth off, believe me, even more than I'd shot my load; in English, Yiddish, pig Latin, jive talk, broken Polish and worse Ukrainian. To parents, teachers, adults in general. I'd--I'm afraid to admit it--I'd called the Satmarer Rebbe--the pre-eminent surviving leader of Hungarian hasidic Jewry and the most powerful rebbe on the continent--I called the Satmarer Rebbe a bohunk.

Nu? "If a man has a stubborn and rebellious son..." I don't know where the Christ I ran across the word "elegy", probably reading about tolling churchbells for my homework, but there was no way I was ever gonna figure out what it meant. We didn't have an English-English dictionary, and the Yiddish one didn't have it, so I asked my father, who I figured knew everything, even in English, "Tatte, vus iz der taytsh an elegy?"

He rolled his eyes and put his cigarette on the lip of the ashtray. "Veist takeh nisht? You really don't know? Just as well, I guess, borukh-a-shem. An elegy, it's an...an expression of sensitivity." He hemmed a second and stubbed out the butt with three or four good shoves. "S'iz a min reaktsiye, a kind of reaction to something. Like," he stuck out his thumb and started snapping his wrist, "A man eats an orange and breaks out in hives, hot er tsu oranges an elegy, farshteyst?"

"Not an allergy," I yelled. "An elegy! E-l-e-g-y! You think I talk English from an accent like you do?"

Bastard. Sinner. How many years did *that* take off his life? Count em down, add em up, bingo he's dead, so go up and get your prize: the complete sheet music, whether you can read it or not, with all the words, to *Got un zayn Mishpet iz Gerekht, The Lord is Just and So is His Judgment.*

"...All the men of the city shall stone him to death with stones." To avenge ourselves for the Three Weeks in the middle of summer when fun is forbidden because we lost our Temple, me and Shmiley went to Big Chief Yukkitup, a joke shop on Tenth Street, and--it was all Shmiley's idea, I swear-- we bought twin whooppee cushions to slip under the carpet in front of the Ark, where our fathers always sat to recite the book of Lamentations. On Tisha B'Av, the black fast of the Ninth of Av when the Temples were destroyed, you sit on the floor of the shul. I had a buck that said dinner and Jewish luck, Shmiley thought they'd blame it on structural faults; everybody knew that Columbus was Jewish, and they'd never hallucinated whooppee cushions back in Europe.

But the Lord gave my father a summer cold, and he sent Khaim Mes up to read instead. It might have been Tisha B'Av, but Khaim was smiling like it was Hitler's yortsayt--it took him a chapter of Lamentations to order a bottle of seltzer, he was gonna show us what it means to mourn. He was the man who had seen affliction, and he had a tukhes the size of a watermelon--we were biting our shirts while he was still in the aisle. Khaim flung himself down, hit both the cushions at once, and went flying through the dust motes in a splatting fanfare, like somebody'd goosed the Mummy--the shul hadn't been vacuumed since Shavues.

Nobody won the bet. Our fathers drove us home at the ends of their hands, locked us into our rooms and barred us from the shul 'til the fast was over. With people like us in the world, my father told me later that night, it's no wonder the Temple was destroyed. With people like me under his roof, every day was a day of mourning. "But it was only a joke," I told him. "We didn't mean any harm." It wasn't that I didn't feel bad about the Temple, I just wished God would have taken it during sfireh, the seven weeks between Pesakh and Shavues when you also can't enjoy yourself. "We can't cry when it's cold out?"

"I'll give you what to cry about. You scared Khaim so, he could have had a heart attack and died. Did you think about that, you and your friend, while you were giggling away in the joke shop?"

"No, sir."

"And you'd have laughed at that, too? If it's funny to scare him out of his wits, isn't it even funnier you should scare him right out of this world?"

I was tempted to say yes, just so he'd slam the door and leave me in peace. Instead, I looked at the floor.

My father tugged his beard. "You hate the Jews, uh? You've got a copy of *Mein Kampf* inside your gemore?" I looked back up, wide-eyed. "Then why in the world would it enter your head to play jokes, practical jokes, on Tisha B'Av, unless you thought dead Jews and a demolished Temple and an exile 'til the end of time was something to celebrate? *A Jew*", and he leaned in towards me, "*A Jew* plays jokes on Purim; on Tisha B'Av the Germans came to Poland. And they were laughing, too." One whooppee cushion and I was Hitler. "If this is how you treat the rest of the Jews, the ones you've got nothing against"--my feelings must have shown in my face--"I'm only glad I won't see the barn-dance when it's my turn to go."

They forbade us to mourn. I wasn't bar mitzvah yet, so it was no big deal, legally. Mendel Efsher, Shmiley's father, held him down while Serel stuffed food down his throat--a salami and chocolate milk float, they had to throw the glass out--just to teach him a lesson.

"...And all Israel shall hear and fear." So plait my payes and call me Brunhilde. Kids in the Bible committed sins-- fucked with the sacrifices, killed Abel, worshipped idols--and *they* were killed, not their parents. Look at Nadab and Abihu, Hofni and Phinehas; King David went after his own, in person. So what the hell, *ikh* hob zikh geshmat, *I* maybe apostasized or something? "I'm the one's been singing Christmas carols," I told the Lord, "And I'm ready to take what's coming to me. Now," before my mother got it, too.

There was no lightning, nothing to carry me home. A beam creaked. I drummed my fingers on the floor, waiting for something to happen, then realized that I wasn't sure if I could do this--it might count as making music--so I stopped and waited some more, blew my nose and rubbed my eyes...I'd have to name my son Shaye now--Sherman--ben Yoine the Parricide, The French Fry Killer from the Yiddish paper Extras. No stinkin cops could touch me, but there'd be two stout rabbis

from the RCMP--dial M for mitsve--to march me into a bezdin,
a rabbinical court, headed by the Satmarer Rebbe.

"Yoine Levkes, you stand accused of patricide through the
deliberate flouting of every mitsve in our Holy Torah. Angels
detailed to your case have uncovered irrefutable proof of:

1) the incessant eating of rock badger;
2) immersion in a mikve while holding a frog;
3) anticipating readings in the Scroll of Esther;
and
4) overturning your table by causing a virgin of Israel, one
   Sabina Mandelbroit, to lie on top of you;

this all in addition to the sins you've already confessed. How
do you plead?"

How did I plead? "Guilty, guilty, guilty," I cried. "But with
an explanation."

"Nu?"

"I...I...I thought the Lord God, Blessed be He, said that the
fathers shall not be put to death for the sons."

"Put to death? Who's talking here put to death?" He turned
to each of the other judges, banging his fist on the table and
laughing in a sort of high-pitched cackle. "Put to death!" He
could hardly sit up. Tears were dripping off the side of his
beard. "The furtive Presleyak knows not the meaning of
heartbreak? The youth with shoyn two pubic hairs and a kaleh
doesn't know from hartsveytik? You're underage to be an idiot!
It wasn't God who killed him, it was you. You were right all
along."

Dr. Mandelbroit entered, yelling, "No guilt, no guilt." The
Rebbe took a pinch of snuff; he sneezed, and Dr. Mandelbroit
vanished, a dying puff from the smoke of iniquity.

"Nu, Rebbe," I asked. "Vus vet zayn? What's gonna be?"

He smiled. "Der aybershter, borukh shmoy, iz khitre vi a
litvak. The Lord is as foxy as a Lithuanian Jew. You will live,
Yoine Levkes, live and be well. But you're a Jew. You will never
forget."

I don't know when it was that Shlufiel, the angel of sleep,
finally got to me, but he didn't even stay 'til the end of my
dream. I was awakened by a whooping rattle from the other
side of the kitchen that sent me off on tiptoe like I'd been shot

from a gun. God Almighty, not my mother, too...No, wait, I could hear crying with the cough. I snuck through the kitchen and put my eye to the doorjamb. She was sitting on the living-room floor, completely disheveled, so far-gone with grief that she hadn't cleaned up from the ashtray she must have knocked over. Her shoulders were bobbing up and down. Once in a while, she coughed.

I wanted to go to her, but I was afraid she'd accuse me, so I just stood in the kitchen and peeked.

She never quite stopped sobbing, but the heaving eased off after a while. A prayer book for mourners lay closed on her lap. She sat for a minute or two, then lit another Black Cat. She exhaled, and in the same voice that she used to order off-brand colas from the Polish supplier, "Riboynoy shel oylam," she asked, "Master of the universe, vus vet shoyn zayn?"

She sat as if waiting for an answer. She stared at the wall; maybe it'd come in writing. Finally she sighed, a little too deeply. She coughed, took a puff, then sighed again, this time like a restless baby.

"Mayn heiliker tatte fleg zugn, My sainted father used to say..." My mother was always talking to herself, usually in quotations. "Mayn heiliker tatte fleg zugn..." She was talking to God or the wall, maybe both at once, telling the story of her life--who was in it and when they died. It was a nervous habit she had. "Mayn heiliker tatte fleg zugn az di mishpukhe shtarbt ale mul fritsatik avek, Everybody's family dies off too soon." Her father said it, it had to come true. When she was a little girl, she lost her mother; a big girl, her father; a grown woman, her husband. She was thirty-two years old and her dreams were like silent movies--anybody she liked was dead. Except, thank God, for her son.

Shaye's family was gone, too, but at least you could blame the War. She didn't even find out about her father until afterwards, from some landslayt who'd made it through. The Germans herded all the Jews into the main square, with her father, the rabbi, at their head. They took his shtrayml and crapped in it, then told him he should eat it. Then they blew his head off--he didn't enjoy his food enough.

Of course, Shaye was already a widower when she met him, but that was different, too. His first wife had always been sickly, Shaye never wanted her; but a promise was a promise, even if he hadn't made it, and his father couldn't afford the shame--never mind the fine--that would have gone with a broken engagement: every day she faded a little more, got a little more insubstantial, until she finally blended in with the air around her.

The War broke out a couple of months after she died, my father took off for Lithuania, and the rest was history. He noticed my mother in Vilna, but they were already in Shanghai by the time she'd convinced him to marry her. He was still brooding over the first one, he had qualms about making children who had no chance of becoming adults. Their eldest died in my mother's womb, and my father took it as God's little joke.

"But I did the laughing--like my belly was a dance-floor for lizards. I was eighteen years old and pure as matse-water; first I killed my mother and then I killed my child." You had to understand my mother's dialect; to say that my grandmother died when my mother was a little girl, nebekh, meant that she died in childbirth. "And I'd still like to know what I did to deserve it." My mother had learned to trust nobody, but that hadn't stopped her from staying innocent--even during the War, she never forgot she was a Jewish daughter and sinned no more than daily life required. And it's not like she was a hunk of cow that never had a chance; my mother was very good-looking, in a smallish way--like a ten year old with a shape--and men, especially the older ones, always seemed to go for her. I'd seen it on the street myself. Kalman Franzoys pinched her one day on the train to Vladivostok and asked her if she'd like to see the ceiling through his hair. My mother, who was not quite seventeen at the time, told him she'd rather see the wall through his pipik.

And Kalman was hardly the first. A Dlugaszower hasid from her town had taken her along with him and his family, at her father's request, when they went to join the Rebbe in Vilna. When she refused to marry the hasid's son--he was a tanner and "smelled like an outhouse in the cholera"--they abandoned her as soon as they got to Vilna. She went straight to the Rebbe, whom Kalman had managed to smuggle all the way from German-occupied Galicia, and he told her that where his people went, she'd go, too. So Kalman probably figured she owed him, sort of. "I might even have done it--why not? Everything else had gone crazy, girls my age were giving themselves practically in the streets to the first man they saw, just to have the chance to have done it before they died"--but Kalman Franzoys was old and ugly and never brushed his teeth, and she'd met Shaye months before. Her refugee girlfriends thought she'd gone nuts--she took one look at him and made up her mind that he was going to marry her. He was such a khnyok, they said, he wouldn't touch her even after they were married--no mikve'd be kosher enough. But my mother was still a girl; what would have been idiocy at the best of times was enough to keep her in line. "Get yourself a boyfriend, Rukhl. Get yourself ten and spit in God's face." But my mother had a reason to watch her behaviour--and who was the fool, anyway? You could put out and put out and put out, and still not have a meal by the end of the day. "I stayed frum," she was saying. "Whether I believed it again before the War was over, I still don't know. But I didn't have any choice." Anybody else who said that about my mother would have been carrying their balls in a shoulder-bag. "And for Shaye, nu, frum was all there was."

She started talking about a father I'd never known, a whole different person from the punctilious watcher who ran my life from behind his counter; a khnyok who'd get so fartift in an inyen, so immersed in a passage of Talmud, that he'd forget to tie his shoes--to sit down, for God's sake--for hours at a time. The look on a Chinaman's face could send him leaping to the bes-medresh he'd just walked out of; it wasn't a Chinese face anymore, it was a living dispatch from the angel of learning, and finally my father had it. And if he *wasn't* on his way from the bes-medresh, he'd leave my mother in the middle of the street without even knowing what he'd done. He knew the streets in Sura and Pumbedissa, where the ancient academies had been, better than the ones in Shanghai; he once stumbled into a pothole two feet deep right outside their room, a full six feet across it was and he'd never even seen it, and sprained his ankle. My mother and--she had to admit it--Kalman, too, managed to blow some of the fog away, the birth of his son got rid of the rest. Back then, he used to talk Aramaic in his sleep;

behind our counter, he was strictly business, and he slept in fits
and starts, like any other merchant.

My mother felt a little guilty for pulling him down to earth
like this, "But if I didn't, he would have been in heaven even
sooner," and she started to weep again.

I watched for a while, trying to keep my crying quiet. My
mother found me on the kitchen floor, dreaming--I can still
remember--of heaven. There was a big shvits there, a steambath,
where all the saints and sages sat wrapped in taleisim, learning
gemore from the mouth of God and singing the *Partizaner Lid*,
the partisans' hymn from the Warsaw Ghetto. Each one was
resting his feet on his children's good deeds, while the deceased
wives waited outside with pails of lemonade. Only my father
had his feet on the floor.

"Khap zikh oyf, hertsenyu, Wake up, darling. You can't
sleep all night in the kitchen." My mother was shaking me
gently.

I rubbed my eyes with the backs of my hands, as if I were
in a crib. "It's ok. I'm not tired, anyway."

"Me neither," said my mother, hugging me tight. "Not as
long as you need watching."

"What time is it?"

"Six-thirty. You were so quiet, I didn't even think to check
on you."

It was pitch black outside. Suddenly my gut went hollow
and I remembered. "Mama, we didn't light last night!"
Chanuka goes on for eight days.

My mother stretched her lips into some kind of smile.
"Oyneyn potur, You're excused before the funeral."

"Potur nor mi-vrokhe," I answered vehemently. "Only
from saying the blessing." I could tell my mother was proud.
"Khaim lit it for us," she said. "Nu, zindele." She was leaning
over the sink, peering through the window. "It isn't snowing,
I don't see any wind. What do you say we go for a walk, just
to clear our heads? It's going to be a busy day."

What was I supposed to say? We couldn't have turned on
the TV even if we had one. I slipped into my father's galoshes-
-Shmiley had brought me my coat, but he forgot the boots at
school--wishing I had a snowsuit that my mother could pull

over me. She took me by the hand and we headed out through
the store.

"Not too bad for this time of year, is it?" We were walking
along Fourteenth Street towards the tracks, away from
downtown. If you looked hard in the dark, you could make out
the grain elevators a few blocks away. "Mrs. Gurfein said it's
supposed to warm up, even be above zero for a couple of days."
It wasn't going to make the ground any softer, but I kept my
mouth shut. My mother stopped and swivelled to face me. She
took my other hand, like she wanted to play London Bridge
with my father's ghost. "We're in trouble, Yoinele." And King
Farouk went on dates. "Worse than you know about." She
raised our hands up level with her shoulders, then let go and
shrugged. "Business in the store--puh," she blew in my
direction. "It wouldn't feed a canary," and my father's sideline
was finished. There'd been a crop failure that year, even Khaim
Mes was selling his furniture by barter, trading it with the
farmers for one of their surplus cars, then trying to trade the
cars to Marty Shain for money. Only the farmers had nothing
for Marty except Khaim's furniture, and that they needed, so
Khaim had six or seven cars now, in his driveway and all down
the block, a Packard and a Morris Minor with hand signals, a
Nash Metropolitan and God knows what else, all on top of the
'37 Dodge that he'd never seen any reason to give up. And
Marty Shain was doing even worse.

This was all common knowledge, but I'd never realized that
it had much to do with our store. We got a five dollar purchase
maybe twice a year--usually Christmas Eve emergencies. "No,
it isn't good. We're alone now, and almost broke. Maybe I
shouldn't be talking like this, but you have a right to know it,
you have to know. There'll be some insurance money, and
thank God we don't really owe. But the business--mayn
heiliker tatte fleg zugn that when the farmer gets fat, he fills
everyone's plate. You understand what this means?"

I nodded. We'd walked about three and a half blocks, as far
as Vlad Rewa's White Rose Service Station, where all the Jews
bought gas: Vlad was a proud CCF'er, so we knew he couldn't
hate us. My mother stopped by the air pump, took the hose
from its rest and started changing the pressure with the little
crank, listening to the bell ring. "We probably shouldn't do

this," she said--she was talking about halakha, not about Vlad-
-"But I like it." Apparently--something else I never knew--she
used to stroll down here sometimes when she couldn't sleep
and play with the air pump. It soothed her, she said. "Nu, we
all have our narishkaytn...Tell me, Yoinele, how long were you
listening behind the kitchen door?"

"I don't know. An hour or so." I could feel myself flushing.

"So when did you fall asleep then? Where in the story, I
mean?"

"When you were talking about how tatte used to be so
fartrugn, so distracted all the time."

"You didn't miss much. You should have come in. I'm your
mother, you know, and the living room isn't a bes-medresh.
You don't have to have a divider."

"I didn't want to bother you." She was looking at me like
she knew I was lying. "And I, I didn't want to cry anymore."
I pushed it out in one long word. The bell on the air pump was
clanging, and I was crying again.

"Shoyteh," she said, crying through her smile. "Idiot,
you're supposed to cry. If I'd known you were listening, I
would have said more, you should *really* find out what you
are." The bell rang again. "Mayn heiliker tatte fleg zugn"--it
struck me that I could say it now, too--"Mayn heiliker tatte fleg
zugn az an orphan has to live from stories. Remember, I was
an orphan from my mother--and that's a complete orphan, you
know the saying--so I know what I'm talking about. Did I ever
tell you how your father, alav-a-sholem, used to sneak into the
western movies back in Poland?"

My mother knew what she was talking about. When word
got out that we were broke, that my father had died in someone
else's shrouds--I think he'd taken a mortgage on my hockey
stick--our comforters took to punching the no-sale button on the
register and dropping bills into the cash drawer. The street
door, the one through the store, was locked for the week;
people came and went through the alley-door off the kitchen,
which we usually used for the garbage, but the connecting door
from the apartment to the store was still open; there were too
many people to fit into our living room, and the store was good
to daven in. Khaim and Dr. Mandelbroit brought a seyfer toyre

from the shul, and we said our prayers in the midst of chocolate bars and rocket radios and Mountie pen-knives, all the stuff the other kids envied me--"The Jew can have whatever he wants"--and that I was never allowed to touch. Cigarette lighters disguised as Roman coins, five-cent panatelas with wooden holders and their bubble-gum imitations, wax teeth and snappy nail-clippers and week-old Yiddish papers--they were all right to sell, but that a Jew should actually want such things--except maybe the papers, which went well on a Friday floor--it wouldn't even enter his head. We put a tablecloth over the soda cooler, and read the Torah off the sliding door-panels. Stepping out of the shminesre, the silent standing prayer, one day, Abie Doktor knocked over a tree of sunglasses that we'd stowed in a corner for the winter. It was as full as it had been in 1953, and I was beginning to get an idea why my father, alav-a-sholem, hadn't been doing so well. From cigarettes and candy you couldn't live, and everything else just sat there 'til the cardboard backing rotted. Even the candy--not only had my father frightened the shkutsim away, it was his good luck that it's illegal for a Jew to sell treyf to a Jew: there was almost nothing for the Jewish kids to buy, so they stopped coming, too, and his problems were solved. "That Mr. Levkes," they used to say.

"Like, I was a Teenage Rabbi."

"Go in there for a couple of blackballs--"

"You can't buy a couple, Nimrod. They're three for a penny."

"Shoot me, I lied. He still makes you take some bittersweet chocolate bar from Pesakh, 1902--and you don't have any choice. If he doesn't want anybody to eat it, how come he sells it in the first place?"

And of course, he was always sending money to yeshivas, hospitals, indigent sages and rabbis seeking donations so they could publish their books. Not to mention the bookstores. In the ten years since we'd arrived in Coalbanks carrying nothing but our pockets, my father had managed to collect close to three thousand books, not one of them in the Latin alphabet. Codices, treatises, supercommentaries and novellae--it sounded like an astronomy class; if an inkdrop burped its way out of a Jewish pen, my father was ready to pay for it. Rabbis drove in from Regina, from Butte, Montana, to consult my father's library, and my mother had already announced that we weren't parting with a single leaf. "Dus kind vet zey, mirshem, tsu nits hobn, Please God, the boy'll find them useful."

Like Amazons to a moyel, ma. If my father would have kept his nose in the air like everyone else, instead of in a book, if he would only have kept his mind on business....My bubbeh would have been a streetcar, my zayde the New York subway, I would have been a kiddie-car and everything else would have been the same--nishtu mer. No more. I'd been hearing it all my life, and now it was come upon me. Poland--nishtu mer; Europe--nishtu mer; family and friends and real food, everything we ever had in the non-existent elsewhere of Europe--nishtu mer: funny comedians, real snow, friendly giants, everything nishtu. And my father, too: a link in a chain, a stage in a process, a stop on an elevator that only goes down. Kiddie-car? I wasn't even a unicycle; I was a mikve, an ambulance in Israel, a communal burden of an orphan. Charity saves from death if you're giving, but oni khoshiv ke-meys, a poor person's as good as dead; my father was no more and my mother and me were nothing. People could visit and tell jokes and wish to see each other on happy occasions, and not even remember to look at us; they could moult with their money and never notice my mother's vacant stare or the cosmic dogwhistle of my smart-ass Yiddish.

"Gimme a fag, fast," I told Sabina. It was the day of the funeral, still; they wouldn't let me nap. You've got to understand, for everybody except the immediate family, a shiva's a sort of dry cocktail party with plenty of leftover food--you've got a mandate to enjoy yourself, to show the mourners how life goes on. So Berel Kucker and his wife--she'd just walked into another door, or maybe kissed a burner by mistake--were showing around their favourite wallet-sized picture, a little card about the size of a driver's licence, with Hitler in the middle on top of a swastika, and the rest of them--Himmler, Goebbels, Baldur von Schirach--flanked around him in columns. Their son, Maxie, who was one of the kids in those Buchenwald pictures, had been caught inside a goy's wife in a trailer; they were saying how the youth of today, with their shiksa-khapping and shaygets-sucht, were doing nothing but Hitler's work, and I told them that paperhanging was nothing to be ashamed of. And nobody said a thing.

"I think I'm dead," I told Sabina. "Or maybe invisible." She told me I was being silly; they thought I was mad with grief. She tapped her purse, moved her irises to the corners of her eyes. "C'mon in the bathroom," she said. "Nobody's gonna notice." We locked the door to make sure.

Sabina offered me the toilet seat, but shiva was shiva--I took the edge of the bathtub instead. She had Buckinghams, my father's brand; they sold well at the Legion and the Saint Regis Hotel, which my mother used to call the St. Jesus, and made everything else smoke like Shirley Temple. "The real taste of a real cigarette"; one pack and your fingers stayed yellow. Poor Sabina had to wrap her face in a towel so no one would hear her coughing. I gagged and turned green and took it like a man.

"You know I can't touch you now." We were fanning our hands and could barely see each other. She nodded and bit back a cough. "But that doesn't mean that I don't want to." Now she smiled. "Don't look at me like that."

"Shh, Joey, they'll hear you."

"Fuck *them*. *I'm* the one sittin shiva, and *you're* all I've got."

Now she smiled for real. "T'es mir epes modne," she said. "You're somehow weird to me."

After *that* funeral, I didn't have much choice. Rabbi Applebaum, the little lame prince of exegetes, insisted on holding a eulogy on Chanuka, even though you're not supposed to, and I could still hear my father screaming about it. I tried to explain that my father wouldn't have liked it, would have walked out if he could have; but Rabbi Applebaum explained to me that he was the only rabbi between us and Edmonton, three hundred and fifty miles, and someone might want to get married some day. "In the consuming pain of his injuries," I tried to talk to him nicely, "Our esteemed rabbi and teacher seems to have overlooked the fact that the path of Grampa Israel leads to no eulogies on the Festival of Lights."

Rabbi Applebaum gave me a filthy look and turned his back on me. He was leaning on a cane, a gumboot with Mandelbroit on the turned-down top dangling from the end of his right leg. "I came all the way from Calgary," he said to the wall. He was letting me off easy; his own two boys had been whacked into slowness. "I wrecked my car and broke"--all of a sudden it was broken--"Broke half my legs to get here--I'm going to deliver a eulogy. And anybody who doesn't want to hear it," he rotated on his left heel like the robot rabbi of the future and breathed garlic into my face, "Anybody who doesn't want to hear it, can go wait in the cemetery. There's a nice new hole to sit in."

You had to feel sorry for him; not only was he Rabbi Applebaum and crippled, he also had a bit of a cold. He was no Jan Peerce when he was healthy, but he could usually drone his way through the Moleh, the God Full of Mercy--the major prayer on behalf of the deceased--without having to stop every three or four words to snort, swallow and make a noise like a hamster. But Rabbi Applebaum was a pro. He didn't sneeze until we'd said Amen. He took a red and white polka-dot handkerchief out of his pocket--three for seventy-nine cents, we used to sell them, too--gave a honk and a shnayts and a spit to be sure, and motioned us all to our seats.

He coughed and cleared his throat again, you can't be too careful. He had one hand on the lectern, the other on top of his cane; he waved his bum foot and grimaced, then started to sway back and forth in little jerks, like a horsie at the end of an air-bulb. "When the doleful dispatch reached me"--I could tell already we were in for a big one--"The woefully detailed dispatch apprising me of How the mighty have fallen, of how in Coalbanks has fallen the mighty man, the glory of the Torah on whom all Israel leans and relies, the man perfect in his righteousness, the mainstay and pillar of all Albertan Jewry, our teacher and leader Reb Yishayohu the son of Rabbi Elimelekh Mendel"--Rabbi Applebaum was speaking in a rhythmic cadence, snorting with every comma, and in a high-falutin rabbinic Yiddish that only me and the Europeans could really understand--"Zatsal, may the memory of the righteous be a blessing; when this shattering fragment ripped my ear, I felt myself as orphaned and bereaved"--"Bereaved from his car," whispered Mendel Efsher--"As if I had just lost a second father, God forbid. It's written that all are the relatives of a sage deceased, all must mourn as if they were his children. Shaye Levkes, zatsal, was bound and attached to us all with cords of love, love I say: love for his Creator, may He be Blessed, love for His commandments, and love, reciprocated love, for the entire Community of Israel in all the corners of their dispersion,

wherever they may find themselves. From the ruins of Poland
to Shanghai, China, to Coalbanks and Calgary and even New
York, the name of Shaye Levkes, zatsal, is known where Torah
scholars meet.   Ten years already he served as unofficial
spiritual leader of this holy community, and for free; he was so
makhmir, so strict about not making a spade of his Torah, that
he even refused rabbinic ordination.   Refused rabbinic
ordination? Who refuses rabbinic ordination? Have not many
great rabbis supported themselves from just such stores as
Shaye Levkes, zatsal, and--to divide the living from the dead-
-his devoted wife, the grieving widow, may she keep on living-
-run right here in Coalbanks? But Shaye Levkes would not even
enter the precincts of possible temptation; he kept his distance
not only from a shokhen ra, an evil neighbour, but also from the
yeytser ho-ra, his own evil impulse--evil in his eyes alone.

    "A giant was here and has gone. Rashi says that while a
tsaddik is in a city, he is its praise, its splendour and its glory.
And now"--he slammed the lectern--"Noflo ateres rosheynu,
the crown has fallen from our head. A voice of weeping is heard
in Coalbanks: Eynenu, mer nishtu, he is no more. And do you
not know that a prince and a great man has fallen today in
Israel? Don't you know? Can't you see? The Dlugaszower
Rebbe himself, may he live long and healthy, the world-
renowned tsaddik, has borne witness to the greatness of Shaye
Levkes, zatsal, the greatness capable of producing--even if it
had produced nothing else--such a son as the broken orphan
who sits before me, an emeser, fartsaytiker yidisher bukher, a
genuine old-time Jewish boy such as once roamed the streets
and alleys, crowded the synagogues and study houses of
Poland, Russia, Lithuania and the rest of Europe in their tens
and hundreds of thousands. The goyim, may their names all
perish, the goyim erect statues, monuments, graven images
and other appurtenances of their canine idolatry; a Jew leaves
behind a son.   And this is his monument unto all the
generations."

    Nobody'd ever talked about me in quite this way before. I
could already hear my mother, next time she got good and mad
at me, opening a mouth: "Horse! Ox! Tombstone!" I ran my
hands over my face, feeling for an inscription; I'd check my
chest before I went to sleep.

"...We say the abbreviation zatsal, may the memory of the righteous be for a blessing, after the name of a deceased, but what does this mean? The memory of the righteous we can all understand, but how is it that it's for a blessing? The holy Torah makes it clear that a blessing is something which is given to a man, sometimes land, but just as often--children. The Lord tells Abraham, 'And I will make you a great nation and bless you'--the memory of the righteous is for their progeny, and each righteous generation is at once a reflecting monument of the last generation and a source, a bubbling spring of virtues which nurtures these same qualities in its own future storehouses and monuments. A man is both wheat field and grain elevator--at the same time, at once and all together.

"On account of our sins, our storehouse has been opened; we are as leaderless as heaps of grain. Thistles grow instead of wheat. It is written that the death of the righteous atones even as Yom Kippur, that it is as efficacious as the ashes of the red heifer. What crimes have we committed, O Israel, to warrant so stern an accounting? What misdeeds must be ours? Oy unto us, that we have lived to see our deeds overtake us! It is also written that the righteous are like the Temple, the Temple whose cleansing we must also celebrate today, God's pledge to the Jews. And just as He removed the Temple on account of our iniquity, so now, when we have no Temple, the Holy One, Blessed be He, reclaims one of the righteous from among them whenever the Children of Israel sin. And who went more among them, among us, than Shaye Levkes, zatsal, the cantor, the scribe, the candy store owner?

"Mipnei khato'eynu, on account of *our* sins, He has taken from us the light of our eyes and enlightener of our fools. I don't say that life is epes a kind of hockey game, that the Master of the Universe looks down and sees and makes the announcement for the penalty box of heaven: Coalbanks, one tsaddik for eating treyf. Life is not a hockey game, thank God; there's no Stanley Cup in the world to come, and Shaye Levkes, zatsal--Shaye Levkes was on a whole other team. I don't say that he was perfect; not even Moses our teacher was perfect, but only that he was perfect in his generation. Look around at yourselves and what do you see? Nobody too good, nobody God forbid too bad--beynoynim, what you call in English the middle classes:

not raw, not cooked, warmed up enough not to make you sick. But Shaye Levkes, Shaye Levkes, zatsal, was a feast, a banquet, a ten course meal of holiness and good deeds, and we, a perverse and crooked generation, we devoured him alive until there was nothing left. Ask for favours, ask for help, cut off an arm and stab him in the heart. We killed him, and if the Lord is khalileh to blame, it's only for His grace, for letting dogs like us into the chamber of the feast until the tables were all despoiled and left full of tsoye and ki, feces and vomit. If God is to blame, it's for setting him down in the midst of this"--he gestured broadly with both hands, slipped down on his bad foot, and, his face contorted with rage and pain, he finally broke down crying. "Tsoye?" he cried. "Hefkeyrus un tsoye, contingency and kuk. And He's left us no dessert." The rabbi limped to his chair and sat down hard.

You could have heard a sign-language choir in the Community Centre. The gentiles, the Jews with lousy Yiddish, were probably still asleep; the rest of us were staring like priests in a burlesque house, too embarrassed or too impressed to do anything but gape. You got the sense that Applebaum'd had some kind of premonition--eight or ten years before--and had been working on his speech ever since, updating here, trimming a little there, until it was as perfect as he could get it--the closest to a big-time funeral Rabbi Applebaum was ever going to come. It had taken everything out of him, and he needed three glasses of water to pull himself together.

He dragged his leg back to the lectern. "You may have noticed," he said in English, "Even those of you who didn't understand, especially those of you who didn't understand"--he gave a little smile--"That I spoke for forty-two minutes exactly. Not forty-one, not forty-three, but forty-two: one minute for each year of Mr. Levkes's life, plus one to represent eternity." Everybody looked at their watches and nodded. An appreciative mmm buzzed up from the crowd--the rabbi hadn't looked at his watch at all. "If the pallbearers will follow me to the casket..." He disobeyed what would have been my father's last wish, and they were making him a hero for it.

My mother didn't even notice. Funerals were always held in the Community Centre--a tradition dating back to when it was still the basement--and she couldn't get over the fact that my father had set up the chairs for his own funeral. "Gevald, gevald!" She didn't shut up all the way to the cemetery. "He was expecting *The Jolson Story!*" I was looking out the window and trying to ignore her as we paused the requisite seven times on our way to the cemetery, always in front of some frum Christmas lawn with Santa Claus, reindeer, baby Yoizele in his creche, goddamned stupid lights blinking on and off in the middle of the day, turkey and stuffing and egg-nog inside-- Christmas made me sick, and I never got any cards. "Merry Christmas, Joey"--my classroom antics were winning me friends- -"Oh shit, I forgot. Sorry, eh? What is it you have, Tshanookah? Well, Happy Tshanookah"--like only Xmas can be merry and bright, and Tshanoo--uh, Chanuka is somehow like a fucking birthday, I mean, every asshole has one. "Don't you guys even get presents?" Yeah, sure; piles of gold and a breastplate of judgment.

Even Mr. Sherbowits, the Latin teacher, who liked me so much that he came to the funeral--he must have got so used to having me around that I started looking normal to him; when he made us all memorize *Adeste Fideles*, he forced me to recite, and then translate, the whole last part of the song like I was Bing Catholic Crosby or something. I managed to get up to "Come, let us adore the..." but I could feel the yarmulke rising off my head, and finished, "Well, you know."

"You know what, Levkes?" he asked. "A transitive verb requires a direct object. Where is it?"

"At the end of the sentence," I replied. "Where you usually look for the verb." A couple of people were laughing.

"You're quite right." He pursed his lips. "And it's..."

"Dominum." The Latin wasn't so Jesusy.

"And does dominum mean 'you know'?"

"No."

"What *does* it mean, then?"

"Jeezis K. Reist!" Shmiley didn't even know that he had the answer. "Do we make you eat kosher? Why don't you baptize him on the spot?"

Mr. Sherbowits was so embarrassed--syntax was his life-- that he didn't kick Shmiley out. He stammered and looked at the floor, and even apologized to me in front of the whole class- -I was still his favourite student, you know. It hadn't even occurred to him. Dumbass Colleen Semple stuck her hand in the air and said she protested my blasphemy and special treatment, and Shmiley yelled out that she didn't have to worry, the only special treatment she'd ever get was a bag on the head. "Make it two, Stan," Greg Ramsay said. "One of em might fall off."

Mr. Sherbowits turned around to the blackboard so we wouldn't see him laughing. Colleen ran out of the room in tears and came back with the principal. "She got what she deserved, Mr. Hamilton. I won't tolerate racial slurs in my class"-- Sherbowits was learning as much from me as I was from him. The principal pulled Colleen back out, and when Wayne Frobisher tried to spit on me in the hall--for a baptism, he said--Ramsay shoved him up against a locker and said that at least I had the balls to stand up to a teacher instead of packing Sheiks in my wallet 'til the wrappers wore off.

We got out of the car, and my mother threw herself into the grave before we could get the coffin down. She was wearing a kerchief, and I let Khaim and Serel pull her out.

I wish I could remember it in order, all the time I spent with Sabina in the bathroom and nobody ever got wise. She knew damn well why I was weird, and that's the way she liked me. The rest of them were so glad not to see me, they didn't even notice I was gone. And if anybody knocked on the door, I'd just make like I was pooing. "Again? And my circumcision should weep in my pocket?" "He can't take the heavy food," Sabina would tell them. We'd take turns going out alone just to keep things kosher, and there were only so many cigarettes you could smoke. We spent enough time in there to develop husky, he-man coughs; enough time outside to overhear Khazkel Baalebos, the big shot real estate man who also sold insurance, whispering to people to stop putting money in the register. "I have an announcement to make," he finally yelled, banging a spoon against the side of his glass. "We should feel sorry for these people, very sorry. But not the way you think."

"Shut up," said Khaim. He was clenching his fists.

"No, I won't. And you can't make me. People deserve to hear the truth." What? My father was Igor Gouzenko, my mother Tokyo Rose? *Confidential*--which we wouldn't sell--was going to do a story, and that's what killed him?

"They have insurance," he shouted. "I sold them the policy." My mother asked him to leave and Serel Efsherke made sure he did so. They went right on laying bills in the little trays. Dead and with the store closed, my father was doing better than he ever had in his life; my mother was a wealthy widow, according to Khazkel, and I was left-handed beneficiary: the cantorial records were all mine. And the books, of course. And the sheets of parchment and quill pens and gallnut ink that stunk up the whole place, a half-finished mezuze and eighty percent of a Torah scroll, not to mention spare velvet yarmulkes, tsitsis I could still grow into and my father's giant-sized, real grown-up married man tefillin--I started wearing them during the shiva. The boxes weighed a ton, even without their solid silver cases, and I led the morning prayers with my chin dug into my clavicle, a heavy woollen tallis over my head, coughing into my chest from the Buckinghams. The coughing--even more, the coughs I managed to suppress--deepened my davening style, lending it a strained glottal kvetch that was straight out of Europe. I sounded eighty-five years old--phlegmy, adenoidal and weeping; an artist of the prayer-stand. Shakhris took about three quarters of an hour, and it hurt me to raise my head before eleven o'clock: there wasn't much doing on the floor, but at least it wasn't my mother. She started sobbing whenever I caught her eye.

They came and went like the tides all week, from Arele Morgenstern with the earhorn to Shelia Koptshinik's new baby, every Jew in Coalbanks and plenty even from Calgary. Goyim, too--neighbours, business associates, kids from my class. Darius Fong came every day, and his father, whose English made *us* sound like Winston Churchill, always came along to help out with the cooking. I never knew I had so many friends. Mr. Sherbowits, my Latin teacher, made a real hit with my mother; he sat and talked with her in Polish--even I could figure out what about--until I started to feel like some kind of quiz kid. He kept looking around at our living room like he was the first white man at Niagara Falls; ninety percent of the people spoke Polish, and Sherbowits couldn't get enough. "You never told me about *this*," he enthused. Nu, a generation comes, a generation goes; I wasn't losing a father, the Jews were gaining a cheerleader. "I never realized they could all speak Polish."

"Only when they have to," I told him. He looked puzzled. "When the children shouldn't understand."

"And what about you, Joey? Czy pan mowi po polsku?"

"Enough," I said in English. "We usually talk Yiddish. With Polish, it's strictly nescio sed fieri sentio."

"You see, Mrs. Levkes," he called out in Polish, and put his hand on my yarmulke, "*This* is why I became a teacher." He could have creamed it and put it in a can, it was nice to see my mother kvell again, and with colour in her cheeks, yet.

The Jews were all biting their tongues. "S'a nerve she's got. Already she's kvelling, her husband's only halfway to heaven."

"Let her kvell. What else has she got?"

"The demi-orphan's worth it?"

"Kvell, shmell. Any port in a storm."

We got up from shiva on New Year's Eve. I washed, changed my clothes and put on a pair of shoes; Sabina came over and we caught up on our homework.

IV

How a hot potato pudding ever acquired supernatural powers is a problem best left to more subtle minds than ours. Learned scholars--natural scientists, theologians, medievalists--claim to have uncovered traces of a now lost continent said to have been ruled by a large rational potato, the sole surviving memory of which is enshrined in the phrase, "The Might has a thousand eyes." But of the supra-rational tuber, we have no evidence but this:

On a Friday afternoon in the winter of 1877, Mrs. Yoshke Furmanovsky, a stout *hausfrau* of Praga-by-Warsaw, opened her oven door and plunged her fork into the kugel baking within, to see if it were ready. Her husband looked forward to nothing so much as his Friday night kugel--indeed, it was one of the great sorrows of Mrs. Furmanovsky's life that he looked forward to the kugel with somewhat more enthusiasm than to certain other Friday night activities. He would rush home from shul, gobble down the whole kugel, along with some chicken and fish, and then fall straight to sleep, in despite of rabbinic injunctions concerning private duties.

Mrs. Furmanovsky, nebekh, tried everything. She put in fewer potatoes, hoping to make the meal lighter, but her Sabbath frock was fancy enough without a kugel tiara. She purchased herbs guaranteed to wake the dead; her husband, nebekh, spent the night in the outhouse. She made the tea extra strong, the soup extra weak, the chicken extra lean, but by the time the weekly glimmer stole into Mrs. Furmanovsky's eye, old Yoshke--nebekh--would be stretched out on the bed, as level and as useful as a bench in the ritual bath.

So Mrs. Furmanovsky decided to avenge herself on the whole cursed race of kugelen in the only way she knew how: whenever she went to test one, she would thrust her fork murderously into the kugel's tender, yielding flesh, twisting it so hard that she could almost hear the hapless concoction screaming for mercy. "Zuln ale kugelen geyn tsu di ale shvartse-yorn," she would mutter. "Let every kugel go to hell. They've ruined my life...I sweat, I toil, I break my back like a slave in Egypt six days a week, and shabbes, instead of a little nakhes, a little pleasure like everybody else, what do I get? A kugel bowl to be washed out with my tears. They say that on shabbes you're supposed to get a neshomeh yeseireh, an extra soul. Nu, how can I get when my extra lies there as useful, as useful vi bankes a toytn, as cups on a corpse. A plague on every kugel, and may the Lord deliver us from them speedily and in our day, amen."

She was otherwise a very nice woman.

And her husband? A purblind tailor with the mind of a goose. Honk, peck, eat; honk, peck, eat; pull a needle through a hole; honk, peck, eat. Shortly after their marriage, Mrs. Furmanovsky began to suspect him of infidelity, so weak and inconsequential was his desire. But when could he have had the time? He spent all day in the shop, which was the front room of their meagre apartment, and he spent all night chomping and shnorkhing. She began to think that perhaps he was punishing her; perhaps she had sinned against him in some way--she had no experience in being a wife--and he was taking his revenge by denying her. She bought potions and philters, perfumes, negligees like the Polish women wore--all they produced was snores. Where some men had such strong evil inclinations as to be veritable mad dogs for the bed regardless of the time of month, Yoshke Furmanovsky wasn't even inclined.

She sought reasons, excuses. A whole week he works from dawn to dusk, shut up in an airless and stifling room--ok, he's too tired. But Friday, Friday when he stops work at two o'clock, goes to the ritual bath, has a little time to relax and a day of relaxation to look forward to--Friday night stuck in her craw. Many women shared her problems during the week, but Friday night? Why else had God invented it? And Yoshke, after she finally found the courage to ask him, on their eighth anniversary, Yoshke merely answered that he ate so well that he could think of nothing but sleep. And that kugel--so heavy and hearty, it warmed him so, that the vapours shot straight up to his brain, telling it to close his eyes so that Yoshke might savour the taste and aroma--undistracted.

"A-nu," said Mrs. Furmanovsky. "From now on, no more potato kugel. It's coming between us. I have my rights as a wife."

"Wife," replied Yoshke, "If you should fail even one Friday night to fix me my favourite potato kugel, you will lose all your cherished rights. Oys wife! I will divorce you forthwith, and then we'll see about your wifely rights."

So Mrs. Furmanovsky, who, when all was said and done, did love her husband, began to hate his kugel. Every Friday afternoon was a war between her, the potatoes and the spices, with Mrs. Furmanovsky always the loser. Loudly she lamented the fate which had kept her from being born in Ireland.

On the Friday afternoon in question, in the winter of 1877, Mrs. Furmanovsky stuck her fork into the kugel with her usual vigour, gave it a twist and gleefully removed it, studying the tines for traces of kugel blood. Disappointed as always, she was about to shut the oven door, when the kugel, with an alacrity shocking in an inanimate object, leapt from the oven straight to the floor, and sank its teeth into Mrs. Furmanovsky's ankle.

Mrs. Furmanovsky was more shocked than pained; the kugel is known for its blunt, yielding teeth, and she had no trouble shaking it loose. Bits of kugel cling to her ankle, but no tooth marks were to be seen. Hungry for vengeance, she kicked at the errant pudding, only to see it leap cackling onto the table, where it sat smugly, humming *The British Grenadiers*.

A woman of valour, this Mrs. Furmanovsky. She grabbed her broom and set after the kugel like a hound to the fox. She cursed, she shrieked, the sound of the broom slapping the floor re-echoed through the kitchen, but the giggling kugel was always one step ahead, baiting her, egging her on in a heimishen, geshmakenem yidish, a down-home, *tasty* Yiddish: "Me ret fun Aleksandr, un oykh fun Herkules," until Mrs. Furmanovsky, no Hercules, threw down her broom and sank to the floor in despair.

Casting her eyes heavenward, "Why me?" she cried. "What did I ever do to deserve this? The rest of the world lives in peace and quiet, while I, Khayke Furmanovsky, am condemned to do battle with a dancing kugel. If potatoes can sing, it's the end of the world. The Messiah must be on his way. Soon all calves will have two heads and a stillborn child will assume the throne. Men will walk on their hands, horses become rabbis, and I...I will be murdered to death in my own kitchen by a kugel from hell."

"And this is how you say thank you?" asked the kugel angrily. It was reclining peacefully in one of the chairs, and fixed Mrs. Furmanovsky in its gaze. "I come here to help you, and this is the thanks I get? Poked like a pig, chased like a thief, and cursed like a Cossack. I've got a good mind to get up and go right now, except that once I'm finished here maybe I can get out of this kugel and go back to the Garden of Eden where I belong. Kugel from hell! A shvarts-yor af dir, lady, I'll give you a kugel from hell!"

Mrs. Furmanovsky's eyelids grazed the ceiling. "Oh my God, it's possessed yet."

"Possessed, shmossessed. If you'd shut up and listen for a minute, you'd understand the whole thing." And the kugel began its story. "When I was still on earth, I was a famous man. The Rebbe of Dlugaszow, perhaps you've heard of me?"

The Rebbe of Dlugaszow? Who hadn't heard of the holy Rebbe of Dlugaszow? A saint, a wonderworker. He made the dumb to speak, the lame to walk, the barren to give birth. It was said that merely touching his walking stick or the hem of his garment was sufficient to ensure a man's prosperity all the days of his life. A dwarf who looked upon the Rebbe's face one Yom Kippur night awoke the next morning a giant.

The Rebbe of Dlugaszow. Sweet-tempered, kindly, modest. He was never known to have lost his temper or to have uttered an angry word. And what people didn't know, didn't hurt them. Once, shortly after his marriage, the future rebbe made the mistake of attempting to explicate certain rather complicated cabbalistic ideas to his wife. She was a simple, pious girl who wanted only to serve her husband, and she rapidly became lost in the chain of emanations he was describing. The young scholar looked at her bewildered countenance and spat in contempt. "The brains of a kugel, that's what you've got." Her tears so affected him that he vowed never again to insult or speak ill of any living creature.

This vow was never broken. But after a hundred and twenty years, when the Rebbe came before the heavenly court, the kategor, the accusing angel, held this one incident up before the Judge as proof that the Rebbe was not worthy of Paradise. What would scarcely have been noticed on any other record was the sole blemish on this one, and as such, deserved to be treated with appropriate severity.

The judge disagreed. True enough, the Rebbe's sin *had* been a grievous one; true enough, his wife was left with a nervous tic for the rest of her life as a result of his outburst; still, he did not merit Gehenna. Rather, the Rebbe's soul was to be returned to earth in the very form with which he had insulted his wife, *id est*, a kugel, and was there to wander about until such time as the Rebbe, in the form of a kugel, was able--kugel-wise--to repair a breach of domestic harmony and thus counterbalance his own sin on the scales of judgment.

"And so," continued the kugel, "Ot bin ikh. Here I am, lady. Your cries have reached the ear of heaven, and it has been decided that the nature of your problem makes your household particularly well-suited to my mission."

"Some kind of help you'll be," said Mrs. Furmanovsky. "My husband will come in, take one look at you and gobble you up before you can say Rabbi Eliezer ben Horkanos, and I'll be back where I started from. Do me a favour and go somewhere else. Go to St. Petersburg and poison the Czar for all I care, just leave me in peace."

"Lady, I didn't ask to come here, so let's try to make the best of it. If I mess up here--straight to hell. And remember, lady, I was a rebbe; I don't *know* anybody in hell." The kugel wept so piteously that Mrs. Furmanovsky finally gave in. What did she have to lose?

The kugel paced the room for an hour or so, wracking its brains to come up with a solution. Paced and wracked and wracked and paced until, "Hey, Mrs.! I got it! We'll scare your husband out of ever wanting kugel again for the rest of his life. We'll make him so scared of kugel, that the merest mention of the word will set him to trembling and begging for mercy. And I know just how to do it..."

Yoshke Furmanovsky found everything in order when he returned from the synagogue that night. The soup was on the table, and just as he was lifting the last mouthful to his lips, his wife brought in the kugel. Yoshke gazed at it affectionately, saliva dripping onto his beard as he prepared to consign it to his belly. He reached over, pulled the bowl towards him, and almost dropped dead of a heart attack when it told him to keep his hands to himself. Yoshke may have been a big makher at home, but everywhere else he was as timid as a rabbit. He would return from his occasional trips to the market with virtually every item offered him--no matter how much it cost or how little he needed it--simply because he was afraid to say no. Their tiny closet was stuffed with samovar-taps, flywheels, pot-lids. So when the kugel spoke, Yoshke cowered in his seat, awaiting further orders.

"I've had just about enough of you and your gluttony," barked the kugel. "Every Friday the same story. Wolf down the kugel so you can avoid your duty to your wife. Well, we kugelen are sick and tired of being made an occasion for sin by the likes of you, and we've decided to take matters into our own hands, so to speak. From this day forth, if you so much as try to swallow even a single morsel of any kugel whatsoever, that same morsel will tear your throat into a thousand pieces and scatter them to the four winds. Furthermore, if word should ever reach us that you have been...remiss...in your duties as a husband, a group of picked kugelen will see to it that you are deprived of your manhood. And remember, Yoshke, there are some things that grow, but don't grow back."

With that, the kugel leapt up, smacked him in the face, and strode over to the window. It sprouted wings and flew off, never to be seen again.

When Mrs. Furmanovsky came in with the chicken, she found her husband pale and trembling. So sickly was he feeling, he averred, that he had lost all his appetite for food. And for food alone. He led Mrs. F. out of the kitchen, and they lived normally ever after.

Nu. How the Rebbe's soul came to lodge in a kugel, which is not, after all, an animate, organic unity, is a mystery that will never be solved. But that it did, and that in so doing saved the married life of Mr. and Mrs. Furmanovsky, this cannot be questioned. I have the story straight from Mrs. Furmanovsky herself, and can see no reason to doubt it. For Mrs. Furmanovsky, the sainted Mrs. Furmanovsky, the Mrs. Furmanovsky who realized her destiny as woman through the agency of a bunch of crushed potatoes to which the proper heat was at long, long last applied--Mrs. Furmanovsky was my mother.

*   *   *

Only one person could have written it--and he had to have it sent to us with the names crossed out and Shaye and Rukhl Levkes penciled in instead. My mother never knew--she wouldn't so much as touch the thing--and it took *me* a month to find out. *Nights in the Mikve* was seven volumes long. "The swansong of European Jewry," it said on the dust jacket, "Three hundred and thirty-one pages per volume--gematria for 'a krikh' or crawl (also gematria for 'a kirkh' or church, but don't let the goyim bother you)--for a grand total of two thousand three hundred and seventeen pages of new and original folktales from the folk who died in silence. Organized by body-part from the toes on up and taking account of the differences between men and women, *Nights in the Mikve* covers the entirety of Jewish life and history, from Abraham--from Adam--all the way up to the present. *All of it*, the bearded face and hairy buttocks of real, unvarnished Yiddishkayt; the whole grand saga, from Cabbala to Cab Calloway, in a pleasant, easy-to-follow style. Buy it now, while you can still read Yiddish."

He was like psoriasis, that Kalman, stuck to me and dead. Dr. Mandelbroit had called L.A. to tell him about my father, and twelve hours later, in the middle of the funeral, Kalman's prostate finally gave out; either that, or he suffered a heart attack, the *Forward* couldn't be sure. But whatever it was, he did it to spite us, even though my father's prostate was probably the healthiest thing about him. "There's your proof, Yoinele." My mother took it personally. "He had to do everything better than your father."

"Then why didn't he do it first?" I had no idea what my mother was talking about. "Nobody dies for a joke, mama."

"You only met him once, Yoinele. He's been promising for years to meet your father on the other side and show him who was right."

"Don't be crazy, huh? It's heresy even to pay attention. It's a coincidence, that's all."

"Coincidence?" My mother looked at me with pity. "Coincidence has nothing to do with the Jews."

It was months before I realized that she was right. Changing the names in that story was probably the last thing Kalman did--"Erev Xmas/56" stood written at the foot of the page--but croaking wasn't enough to protect my father's funeral. "A terrible thing, Yoine." Sam Rosen, the Manischewitz agent from Calgary, had been there, too, and he gave me the secret details. Forget about Kalman--him we didn't hear about until after--it hadn't been much of a week for anyone: Sam himself had driven Rabbi Applebaum up to Vulcan, where the rebbetsin was waiting to take him home in their car. The rabbi took his cane back to the drugstore and picked up his deposit, and Mrs. Applebaum, who had the eye-sight of a blues-singer when she remembered her glasses, drove straight into the back of an oil-truck, killing the two of them on contact.

"And right after your father like that, it's like we did something, or something." All of a sudden, they were worried; people with pork-chops in their fridges wanted to check their mezuzes, but with my father and Applebaum both elsewhere, all they could do was pray. "When Flaum"--the rabbi from Edmonton, another Chanuka eulogizer--"Started talking--it was what, two, three days after your father? It was like summer re-runs in the middle of Christmas. The Bible, the Rashi, the hockey game--word for word what Applebaum said here." Nobody from Coalbanks had been at the rabbi's funeral; they were too busy with my father's shiva, and they all hated Applebaum, anyway.

"Flaum turned all red when I told him about it. Turns out that him and Applebaum both subscribed to something called The Holzhacker Pen Club--I even wrote it down so I'd remember the name. They get a dozen sermons a year, six in Yiddish and six in English--Canadian and American versions, yet--and that was the one for famous scholars, like anyone who needs it is ever gonna be maspid a famous scholar...Gimme a coupla White Owls while you're back there." My mother had a toothache, thank God, and had left me in charge of the store while she ran over to the dentist for an hour.

"Holzhacker?" I asked, handing him the cigars. The forty-two minutes must have been a happy coincidence; the rest, some unspeakable plot.

"That's right. Some old-time Jewish writer, does this as a sideline so he won't get scurvy. And I'll tell you, it's even better the second time around."

I hoped they'd used it for Kalman. "Do me a favour, Mr. Rosen."

"Mm?" he asked, nursing a stogie to life.

"Don't ever tell my mother."

She was still talking about poor Rabbi Applebaum, may his merits protect us--she'd forgotten already how much she never liked him--and how he'd given everything a man can give to send my father off in style; the first accident, the ankle, the fatal accident, they were all proof that the sitreh akhreh, the sinister Other Side, had wanted my father's holiness to go unmourned by the masses.

And she was still mad at Kalman about the television set. *Nights in the Mikve* arrived with a console the size of a Cadillac--real wood, yet--with a Yiddish broadside taped over the screen, according to which--"The Arch-Patriarch of All Impurity," it was called--a six year old boy of Brooklyn, that city and mother in Israel, had attempted to decapitate his sleeping father because he'd seen them cut a man's head off on TV and then put it back again.

"They should have cut off *his* head," my mother didn't mean the kid, "Sometime before he was born." She spat on the set and forgot about it. I begged her, I screamed and pounded my fists like she was buying me Cream of Wheat instead of the cereal with the prize inside. She spat again and put an ad in the paper.

"Bastard." I'd hear her outside my room at night. "You think you can hide from me? I know what you're thinking." Halevai, utinam, would that she did--I was the only kid on earth who wished he was a TV. "I didn't have anything to do with it." She'd take off a slipper and throw it to the floor. "And I'm still your mother, whether you like it or not."

Go argue with a refugee. We could have been waiting for a minyan to say kaddish, if I was five minutes late getting home--and this was after she'd phoned the shul, the Mandelbroits, the Greenbergs and The Number One Son Chinese and Canadian, even though she'd already got me on the call to the shul--five minutes late and she'd lock herself in the bathroom for the rest of the night. Thank God, they had alleys in Alberta. I invented so many stomach-pains to get her out of there--"Oy mama, di blindeh kishke, di one-eyed mouse, I'll have to hock my intestines and kuk in the creek"--that I started to feel them for real. Dr. Mandelbroit understood the bellyaches, but my mother was a different problem. "You know as well as I do what she needs." He talked to me like I was an adult, and I should never have told him to go fuck himself--I think it gave him ideas. Miss Dehmel, the social worker, wanted me to find my mother a hobby, but all I could suggest was goy-watching. The Dlugaszower Rebbe--I wrote him in New York--he had the same idea as Benoit, but for different reasons. We were sitting pretty, after all. From the shiva alone, we realized the gematria for "as an inheritance", $523, along with two English pennies; the insurance money--like twenty thousand dollars, gematria for "lemme at her"--would be coming through any day, and don't forget selling the TV. My mother was some catch, all right, you could almost forget about Coalbanks. She looked ok, too, and you never know--maybe it was only half her fault that I was an only child.

I couldn't see her having any more, though. Not if she kept sitting up to three and four in the morning, talking to the picture of my father on the living room wall. He couldn't tell her much about business and he had no idea what to do about me, so they talked about Shanghai. I don't know what my father was telling her, but Shanghai was looking good to my mother; Shaye wanted to meet her there.

I phoned the Dlugaszower collect in New York, and told him to get out here before my mother did herself a deed. I was starting to fail Latin already.

"Check the mezuze, Yoinele." He told me which Psalms to say, when and how often. He told me to lay a kvitl on my father's grave, a prayer-note with my request inside it, and to wake up before dawn and say the Chapter of Song.

He was the kugel's great-grandson, you know; miracles ran in the family. Miss Dehmel had consulted Dr. Mandelbroit about the most recalcitrant case she'd ever seen--"They think they were *commanded* to be freaks"--and Mrs. Mandelbroit moved back to Calgary as soon as the school year was over. She took Genia with her, and Sabina lost her taste for petting. She started sleeping over on our couch--"I can't even look at him, Joey"--and no monkey business allowed.

You would have thought my mother had just lain in; she was so caught up with Sabina's immortal soul and household strife--she even taught her how to take khaleh--so encouraged that she and my father really *had* been living right, that she started singing *Get Over Here, Philosopher*, an old hasidic folksong, and finally remembered that dying isn't all that can happen.

By the beginning of my sophomore year, when the Mandelbroits finally made up, my mother was as much herself as she'd ever be again, and I was winking at Miss Dehmel every time I passed her in the hall. My father had been dead for nearly a year.

Sabina was beginning to thaw out again--I tried to explain to her that broads like Miss Dehmel had a certain, how do you call it, *effect*, on all healthy males, and that she shouldn't take it personally--and the day I could dance and listen to music and go to the movies again, she decided that she could touch. First *Bridge on the River Kwai* downtown, then back to Sabina's for a mambo marathon and a couple of waltzes to *La Vie en Rose*. My feet were still tapping when we hit the couch, and I ended up with three fingers inside her, working them 'til she was dripping like a diaper. I smeared her juice onto my right thumb, my right ear-lobe, the big toe of my right foot--like the High Priest with the blood of a sacrifice. I didn't have the nerve to recite the liturgy, though, and Sabina got mad at me for clowning around just when we were both getting back to normal.

Nobody died for a while. I got a trophy and a Vulgate Bible for winning the Alberta Latin Contest, and my mother put the trophy in the window of the store; the Bible's probably still in my locker. We were getting on a little bit better, and the only time she hit me, I deserved it. She told Mrs. Clancy, the old Irish lady who used to come into the store, how much she, my mother, dreaded being alone for her orgasm--I'd told her it means middle-age. She punched me so hard I got a black eye.

Then it started all over again. Khaim Mes, Abie Doktor-- thank God, I'd finished saying kaddish and didn't need a minyan to daven--and worst of all with Shifra Dropdead.

Shifra Dropdead hadn't put on a girdle since 1939, but for your daughter's funeral you put yourself out. It's the least you can do if she won't be getting married. But after nineteen years Shifra was a little out of practice, so she sent her Khaykele, the dead one's twin, to get my mother to come tug the thing over her bulges. "And you don't know how?" my mother asked. The girl shrugged her shoulders. "She asked for you."

She didn't have much choice. The way Shifra used to kvetch and bray you'd have thought she had a tapeworm in her brain; at a time like this, when you need somebody to talk to, she was lucky to be able to talk to anybody at all. Figure it this way: you're an aguna, an abandoned wife, in a small town in western Canada where the only single Jewish men are over seventy or waiting for their driver's licence. And if there *was* anybody eligible...Between the War and your husband's desertion-- especially if he takes off for Vegreville two days after the birth of your twins and refuses to come across with a Jewish divorce even after the whole town takes up a collection to pay him off- -you're left with a feeling that everybody from God on down is out to get you. You're forced to make a living the only way you know how--selling fresh eggs door-to-door. Your pristine temper, which was nothing to write home about anyway, takes up with your new-born misery and paranoia to produce some miscreant hybrid of Pascal and Oscar Levant, so that when you charge down the street with your baby-buggy full of eggs the crap gushes out of you like oil from a derrick. "Whining bastards; Ukrainian pigs and yiddishe klipehs, let your bacon run naked--kill me again. Ha! I've got a toenail suffers more than you do. You wanna weep? Weep to me, you buggers. Tell *me* how hard you got it; look me in the face with your millions of tsuris, *look me in the face* and go drop dead!"

Plus you're ugly on top, dumpy and low-slung--"You see her?" Khazkel Baalebos once asked me. "She's suing the city. They built the sidewalk too close to her ass"--with hair like a pot scrubber and a blotched, bleeding face like the insides of a pomegranate. Add it all up, figure it all together, you'll never get the prize for Miss Congeniality.

Not that she was much of a social butterfly to begin with. She was like any other D.P. at first. Quiet, suspicious, a little bitter around the lips--who could blame her? And a husband--no husband but a killer. He'd gone Canada-sick; he wanted to be a millionaire and sleep with stewardesses. She didn't have it easy. One day she got pregnant. Another day Herschel kicked her in the stomach and she lost the baby. The day after she came home from the hospital, Shifra showed up in our candy store and bought every piece of penny candy in the place. She borrowed my little red wagon and off she went, up and down every street of that stinking little town, dragging the wagonful of wrinkled, drooping bags, stopping every time she saw a kid, anything that hadn't hit puberty yet, and tearfully offering it a piece of candy. About one percent of them took. Shifra was that ugly. My father offered to buy it all back, but she just went on walking; when the local paper tried to celebrate the advent of the Candy Lady, Shifra told them, maybe the first time she ever told anybody, to drop dead.

It got to be a habit with her, this dropping dead, especially after Herschel finally took off for good. "Drop dead, drop dead, drop dead"; meaningless, a nervous tic--but try and tell her victims. Customers, passers-by, her neighbours in the shul--she dropped them all dead. If she'd been God, there wouldn't have been a human being left alive except herself and her twins, a couple of plump little blondes who looked like a pair of shabbes chickens. Them and my mother--most likely because of my father. As soon as the shiva was over, Shifra took to hanging around our store like they'd just abolished money, engaging my sainted mother in filozofye.

"Life, Mrs. Levkes, who needs it?" she'd ask, jamming a Sweet Cap where her front tooth should have been.

"They say it's for the living."

"Better," Shifra would reply, "Better they should give it to those yet unborn...It's like a harem, this life: you enjoy yourself once and then wait for them to carry you out."

My mother would nod and wipe a tear from her eye. "A kholyera afn malekh-a-muvehs, A cholera on the Angel of Death, Nor ver vet zi im gebn, But who's going to give it to him?"

Who do you figure? But He's biding his time until the end of the seder, while we sit here trying to fidget our way through the fir kashes. Until the malekh-a-muvehs gets what he's so good at giving out; until the Holy One, Blessed Be He, plants His heel in the neck of death and my father, may his memory be blessed, rises from the grave and opens an undertaking parlour, there's no help for it. It should only happen to others.

"Yoinele," my mother said after Khaykele had left, "Promise me on the soul of your father, alav-a-sholem"--as if that left me any choice--"Promise me that from now on whenever you're crossing the street, you'll look both ways *twice*, and then say a shtikl toyre while you're going across." That explained the invocation. Khavele had been run over by a car, and everybody knows that the Angel of Death can't touch you when you're learning Torah. King David staved him off for years that way. Aren't the old folks' homes stuffed with Russo-Japanese war veterans afraid to go to sleep lest they get caught between a snore and a Psalm? So I gave her my promise. "And also," she added, "Be extra careful. Remember, from Labour Day to New Year's, they're"--and she didn't have to tell me who they were--"They're drunk all the time. Their Christmas season," she explained. "When you don't have any mitsves, it's the only way to celebrate." I told her not to worry. I had no intention of doing any of it, but I figured my mother had enough tsuris already.

She came over and put her hands on my shoulders. "Shoyn dervaksn, full-grown already," she murmured. I was edging towards five-feet-one. "Neshomele, soul of mine, once was enough; I couldn't bear to lose you, too. Look at Shifra. Every day she lives is one less day to suffer, and from now until she goes she'll count the days the way the goyim number their years. One after Khavele, two after Khavele, and on and on until they finally call her, too."

"But what about Khaykele?" I asked. "She doesn't count for anything?"

"Count? Of course she counts. But one twin without the other...Tell me, Yoinele, what can one shoe give you but a limp?"

"And the girdle, she couldn't put it on herself?"

My mother pursed her lips. "S'a oysgelassener bisti, you're such a debauchee."

"How debauched?"

"You know how." It was the girdle. It wasn't becoming in the mouth of a youth, or at least not a male youth.

"Ok. But she still couldn't do it herself?"

"Thank God we're alone; for a smart boy to be so stupid sometimes--when were you born? Last night? It isn't so much that she"--it had to be she, Shifra Dropdead being disrespectful and her real name, Mrs. Tregger, ridiculous already--"It isn't so much that she needs help with her, uh, help getting dressed, as it is that at certain times..." the door opens and in walks Shifra Dropdead herself, wavering uncertainly between the oy-veys of the last twelve hours and those of the rest of her life.

She was wearing a black dress and a thimble-shaped black hat that had probably been jaunty until she tore the fake fruit out. Her stockings were unhooked, rolled so tightly around her ankles that they looked like donuts, and from her outstretched right hand dangled the gravest contradiction of my mother's judgment I'd ever been lucky enough to see. Shifra Dropdead hadn't put on a girdle since 1939, but what she had in her hand would have been getting a pension even then. It was a girdle for Bernhardt or Lily Langtry, a jumble of laces which had to be pulled and hooked up from behind, with the helper's foot somewhere deep inside the wearer's tukhes; it was a girdle for Queen Victoria or a barroom hootchy-kootchy, and no child would have been strong enough to heave it shut.

My mother was no child, thank God; half-right was still better than nothing, and in a world like this one you took whatever you got. She flicked her head at the girdle. "Un dus, an oondenk der bubbens, a souvenir of your grandmother?" For all the good it did, she could have yelled "Fresh fish"; Shifra stood staring like a carp on a plate. Finally she muttered. "Hurry, it's almost time."

I never saw what went on in there, but from the grunts and sighs I heard while putting on my suit, the muttered curses and gnashing of teeth, it must have looked like one of those French postcards I'd heard so much about, except that Shifra, whom I imagined getting redder and redder while my mother puffed and tugged like the Volga boatmen, Shifra was getting ready for a funeral and not for Maurice Chevalier. "Keep pulling, Mrs. Levkes." My mother's biceps and calves were bulging, they quivered like those of our fathers in Egypt. "If it wasn't for Khaykele," my mother told me she whispered, "I'd do myself something."

"God should protect us from such things," my mother groaned.

"Let him try," said Shifra. "If we have to be holy because He is, we can stop being so holy already and start acting more like Him. If you eat pig, you might as well lick your lips." If God could make sins, so could Shifra--just let Him see.

I was sitting on my bed waiting for them to call me when the house gave a shudder like a sinner on Yom Kippur, and in place of a sigh I heard my mother scream Shifra's name. I blessed the Lord, whose sages had decreed that the requirements of feminine modesty don't override the saving of a life, and burst into the living room with the zeal of a jealous husband. Shifra was sprawled on the floor like a toppled idol, with Khaykele kneeling and weeping at her side. My mother was pacing back and forth, never taking her eyes from the picture of my father on the opposite wall, and the girdle was hanging over the shade of our floor lamp, a good six feet from either my mother or Shifra. The laces were hanging below the shade in a nice little fringe, and my mother was grumbling in time to her steps. "Not in this house. Never, not for nothing. Far dem iz ken teyrets nishtu, there's no excuse for it."

"Oysgegan?" I asked, pointing to Shifra, "Kicked off?" figuring that my mother was inveighing against the vagaries of providence.

"Nisht toyt, nor tippish," she answered. "Not dead, just stupid."

This was a big relief. "And the girdle--her thing--geplutst? It burst?" But I was beginning to wonder.

"I let it go."

The fact that my mother had put up with Shifra all these years was enough to show that she wasn't cruel or malicious. "What'd you do that for?"

She told me, and I couldn't blame her. While Shifra was chugging along with her invective, cursing God and man and Hitler and God and God and God, until she finally got to the point where she was determined to show Him just where to get off, that she could be just as mean and petty as someone who owned a universe, she threw back her head--which wasn't hard, since her gut was already parallel to the ceiling--and gave a shray to rend heaven and earth. She called God by His real name--the one that only the High Priest utters once a year in the Holy of Holies, and we haven't had a High Priest or a Temple for two thousand years--she called God by His real name and told Him to go drop dead.

The drop dead my mother could have taken; the woman was distraught, after all. But the Shem Ha-Mefoyrash, the Ineffable Name--this was takeh too much. She was so shocked that she threw her hands over her ears, the girdle--which had already started creaking--went flying across the room, and the wayward Shifra was immediately brought low.

By the time I'd heard all this, Shifra had made it back to her feet and pulled her dress down over her head. As she was about to open the door, she stopped and turned around. Her face was redder than I'd ever seen it, and she'd bitten all the way through her lower lip. "You're still coming, aren't you?" she asked my mother. My mother gave a rueful smile and nodded yes. "Thank you...A rakhmunes afn kind," she moaned. "A pity on the child. I didn't want to embarrass her, and now look at me." She slapped her tukhes so hard that her breasts started wobbling inside the dress. "Khavele, Khavele mayns. I've struck matches that lasted longer than you did." She turned back and opened the door, pushing Khaykele out ahead of her, then called over her shoulder, "And you, Mrs. Levkes, hurry up or you'll be late." My mother glanced at her watch and nodded. She wanted to know if I was ready, but I was already staring out the window in my suit, watching Shifra waddle down the street, her body weeping with fat, her backside rubbing against her dress like an ox against a wall.

"Mama, I need to talk to you." I bopped my shokl on the off-beat by Purim of my junior year, intoned my Torah with the fifths all flatted every Monday, Thursday and Oo-bop-a-shabbes. It was meshiekhs tsaytn for us high school shmoes; the world was going beatnik, and you didn't have to be good in gym. Nine times through *On the Road*, and I still didn't get it; if goyim getting drunk was the wave of the future, then the Yiddish papers were hip, as hep to the shlep as they come, but I wasn't going to argue with success: secret admirers were wooing Genia Mandelbroit with valentines of bongos, and compared to a plain old yarmulke, my new black beret was the bendin, solid-sendin, the all-offendin, nisht far ka yidn gedakht, livin' END. I swung with my tsitsis, flipped my Little Bo-Payes into beat generation sideburns while scatting my daily gemore to *A Night in Tunisia*. I was driving my mother insane.

"A beret in mitske drinen?" You have to pronounce the "t". "A yarmulke isn't good enough?"

"Oy, mama, man, heng mikh nisht oyf. Don't hang me up with the yarmulkes." I could have had berets on my feet, I'd never have talked to a kid like this.

"I'll hang you up on the wall, you Hipnik! I had to tell them today at the school"--my mother could never remember the name--"I had to tell them today that you're still called Jonasz." She pointed at the telephone like it was contagious. "I had to tell them my son's a liar, the tragic error never took place, that in no language know to man does Yoinele really mean"--she went over to the pad by the telephone where she'd written it down--"Bobby isn't good enough?" She tore the paper into little pieces. "You had to tell them you name means Jelly Roll?"

She slapped me before I could say Bird Lives. Ever since the Latin contest, they'd been watching themselves at Major Douglas; they didn't really believe my name-change, but after the stink when they didn't really believe that I couldn't go to Edmonton and write the Latin contest on a Saturday, they weren't taking any more chances. I'd come home from school in tears; when my mother heard what had happened--I'd qualified as the Coalbanks contestant and been disqualified for keeping shabbes--she was on the phone to the *Frontiersman* before I could finish. "Jewish Student Can't Win," read the headline; this was Coalbanks, remember, and I made the front page, two payes and a nose. In the article under my picture, Mr. Sherbowits declared that I couldn't lose, and the *Frontiersman* reminded its readers that Major Douglas hadn't even won a football game since the Spanish Civil War.

The principal said it was out of his hands; the contest and its rules were set by the province. Two more editorials and a couple of phone calls, and the province knew better. Two rabbis, a Hebrew school principal, the combined Alberta B'nai B'rith, three Catholic priests, an Anglican bishop and a metropolitan who ordered egg matses from our store sent a petition; the story got picked up in Calgary and Edmonton, and the Ministry of Education arranged for me to stay with Rabbi Flaum and his sermon-books, I shouldn't starve to death in Edmonton before I won the contest. Sherbowits was right, I couldn't lose--without being lynched. He came with me as chaperone and coach; we spoke Latin for eight hours on the train and he spent the weekend talking Polish with the rabbi, who got his picture taken with his hand on my head, blessing me as I went in to write the contest on Sunday.

I could have won the Nobel Prize for Ablative Absolutes, they would have held it against me at Major Douglas. I wouldn't fit in and I didn't flunk out; right after my father died, my mother discovered the telephone, and her non-stop shit-disturbing was the lodestar proof of familial maladjustment that kept me sitting in Miss Dehmel's office like a fruitcake waiting for Christmas. The Latin contest only confirmed what they'd decided when I had to start taking German the year before--my mother was even crazier than I was.

"What's this, Yoinele?" My mother disapproved of the German textbook. "It's like you can't already speak it?" All European Jews--and their Asian-born progeny--talk German like Nathan the Wise; up until the War, it was a well-known fact that the Germans were nice people who were being murdered by their language, and there was no such thing as a Jew who couldn't speak it.

I told her I didn't have any choice if I wanted to go to college. "Tell me, Mr. Hamilton." My mother screamed 'til they got him out of the meeting. "My English isn't so good, maybe I didn't hear--we *lost* the War?"

They upped me to three sessions a week for a while, the final hour reserved for my mother, and damn near kicked me out of school with Shmiley as punishment for our partisan actions against Frau Zimmer. The bitch of Brunschweig, known throughout Major Douglas as The Fraulein--as in, "Keep away from"--was also rumoured to be Hitler's lost twin sister. It was the hint of mustache that did it.

"They signed an armistice, you heroes." I'd never seen Mr. Hamilton so mad. "And don't ever forget it again. Frau, uh, Mrs. Zimmer is as good a Canadian as you are, and I won't put up with this kind of prejudice. Especially coming from *your* glass house. Clapping when she mentioned the bombing of Dresden! It doesn't matter *what* you think, there's such a thing as simple good taste."

"That's what I thought it was," said Shmiley

"What's that, Greenberg?"

"Well, if we're all on the same side like you said, sir, then she should be just as glad about it as we are."

"Don't get smart, Greenberg. You're in enough trouble already." I can't remember if we'd been humming *Die Fahne Hohe* or the *Horst Wessellied*. The principal leaned over his desk. "Maybe you guys think Hamilton's kinda dumb, maybe you think he's a bit of a, what do you call it, a bit of a square?" He smiled like we were supposed to, uh, dig this. "And maybe I am"--I wanted to put an arrow in his suspenders--"But explain to me--and I'm asking as a friend, not as your principal"--my enemies should have such a friend--"I just can't understand why you sign your papers *Judensau*. You kids find this funny? Really, I just don't understand. You think your parents would laugh? And you, Levkes, what do you mean by submitting a sight composition called *Die Juden Sind Unser Ungluck*"--his voice was rising so high, it sounded like he believed it--"Alleging that the German class would be a better place--and roomier--it you weren't there?"

"I thought she'd agree--"

"She? Who's *she?*"

"Ayesha?"

"What was that, Levkes?"

"Sorry, sir. Yiddish. It means excuse me."

"Go on."

"I thought Mrs. Zimmer would agree with me. And I *did* get a hundred percent."

"Nobody's complaining about your marks, Levkes, but get this through your head--and you, too, Greenberg. Without your German credit, you can both sit here 'til the year 2000, you're not going to graduate, and you're not going back to German until you apologize to Mrs. Zimmer--and she decides to accept. So wise up"--he slammed his desk, then sat back to study the expressions on our faces, "And I don't want to hear *anything* about *either* of you *ever* again."

He should have lived so long. Sure, we started to behave--university was the fastest way out of Coalbanks. We wrote a *Verzeihungsbrief* to get back into class, but Frau Zimmer still couldn't win--she had to present me with the German prize at the end of the year, an inscribed copy of *Faust* in old-fashioned printing, while the band played *Ach Du Lieber, Augustin* and I gave my thank-you speech in Yiddish.

"But I'm of German descent myself, Joey." Miss Dehmel and I were like old friends by this time, so when I hit her with a couple of Hitlers, she knew they were only for form. Getting fucked by Dr. Mandelbroit hadn't done her much good, and even a year and a half later, long after the German thing had blown over and been forgotten--Frau Zimmer *liked* me by grade eleven 'cause I spent the summer reading *Faust* and started signing my papers Joey "Gescheiter als alle die Laffen" Levkes, like I was Clark "Superman" Kent--long after I'd made the Germans into my allies, Miss Dehmel and I were still spending more time on her remorse than on my mother and me put together. She just couldn't get over what she'd done with Benoit; her peaches and cream complexion had hardened to a bloodless brick cheese, and she had the scar on her cheek where Mrs. Mandelbroit clawed her. Benoit made the first move, she told me, but nobody cared, not even her. She didn't even care about his motives, or what he could have done instead--it just

wasn't the same Miss Dehmel. And the way she was dressing-
-I could have told her that I dreamed I saw Joe Hill last night
eating my mother and me on Yom Kippur--I was still stealing
material from Dr. Mandelbroit, the world's foremost Paul
Robeson fan--I was lucky to get bare ankle; I could stand up in
her office whenever I wanted.

"I blamed you for a while, Joey." I tried to tell her she was
crazy, that I didn't really care what she did, that nobody would
ever have been the wiser if Benoit'd had the brains to pick a
Christian-owned motel, but Miss Dehmel, who was seeing a
social worker of her own by now, was so wracked with guilt--
"Why didn't you tell me your girlfriend's name?"; so convinced
that her illicit sex life had turned me into a beatnik; so hung up
on Benoit after all this time, that she could think of nothing but
reparations. She wanted to do something nice for me and
Sabina. I told her to forget about it, all was forgiven, she could
stop crying when I mentioned Sabina's name, but Miss Dehmel
was too busy picking her scabs. She must have distilled two
years of notes about me into the one secret desire she'd always
known I had, then gone to Mr. Hamilton and convinced him to
hold the junior prom on a Thursday, so Sabina and I could
attend.

When I reminded Miss Dehmel about dancing and Jewish
law, all I got was a hand on my shoulder--I'd been immune for
months already--and a "Try, Joey. You owe yourself a little
fun."

I owed myself something, all right, but I think it was a
punch in the mouth. I told Miss Dehmel the truth about Jewish
law because I enjoyed watching her waver between numbed
incomprehension and patronizing pity. Everything else was
made up or hushed up--I'd never even told her that the
Mandelbroits *had* a basement, let alone what went on down
there--and she thought she was going to expand my horizons.
She almost fell out of her chair when I didn't recognize the lilies
on her desk. "Nu?" I asked her. She loved when I lapsed into
Yiddish; it was so...unselfconsciously authentic. "They're
good for the Jews?" "Poor Joey, you've got so many problems."

Like if one Jew farts, we're all addicted to beans. To balance
my own deficiencies and keep Miss Dehmel out of the Nazi

party--she used to quiver for the non-human, Miss Dehmel--I made the traduced and abused Sabina, the girl--as I never failed to point out--who had yet to recover from her father's slip and had no chance to discuss it with the social worker--I turned Sabina into Reva the kosher Bird Girl, the eldritch belle of the chicken preserve who kept leaves in her dictionary and let me hold her hand as often as twice a month. "It's forbidden, you know, even to touch a woman who isn't your wife." Miss Dehmel would smile and put her hand on my shoulder. *Sabina*, the real Sabina, wouldn't go near a sparrow for fear of disease; she was allergic to pussy-cats and afraid of a house-fly. And demanded constant physical attention.

"Aren't you exaggerating just a little, Joey?"

"When it comes to halakha"--Miss Dehmel was picking up on my language--"I don't need to embellish."

I had no one to blame but myself, and a punch in the mouth would be getting off easy. I could tell Miss Dehmel whatever I wanted, but I'd never lied to my mother about me and Sabina. Holding hands really is forbidden, and going out with Sabina was like returning from the army with a tattoo on my arm that said Babe--my mother never asked so she wouldn't have to know. Which left me with nothing to appeal to if I wanted to go to the prom. "Aw, but ma"--I could hear myself wheedling like Wallace Beery--"You think I never kiss tit?" I'd be kissing floor to get my teeth back.

On the other hand, I felt a certain obligation to the beatnik international and boys with payes everywhere; high school dances aren't so square if you have to live by the *Shulkhan Arukh*, and I'd never in my life heard a real live band.

So I wandered into the store that afternoon, my beret carefully tilted so the yarmulke wouldn't show, and gave my mother a try. "Like, mama." She was sitting behind the counter with her arm in a cast, listening to Shifra Dropdead's laments. The women's balcony at shul had collapsed during Dave Levinsky's wedding, and my mother was the only casualty. "Like, mama, I need to talk to you."

We'd had plenty of practice since my father died, and reached absolute no in less than five minutes. But I owed myself some fun. I was fifteen years old and had a mouth like a hand-grenade; when my mother told me what she always told me, that the Torah was our life and the length of our days, the pin fell out. "The length of our days, mama? Ask the tatte about length of days. Or your father."

She reached across the counter and slapped me.

"And for *your* father, nothing?" Shifra asked.

"We both ignored her. "Kik, mama, look." I ran my hand along my cheek. "I'm a man already." And my nails had joined the Ice Capades. "I, I've got hair where no one can see."

"And you started a fire with the magnifying glass? Mazl tov, Smokey the Bear--you couldn't just rub two sticks?"

"We could rent him out Chanuka"--God, I hated that Shifra--"The first night, anyway."

"Mama! Shut her up!" I was losing my beatnik aloofness.

"Enough with the mama already. You'll do what I tell you to do."

"But--"

"Don't say anything. I already know how you pee, Mr. Grown-Up Man."

If I'd only asked Miss Dehmel what a motel room was like, none of this would have been happening. "And I'll--I promise I'll spell Rukhl bas Tevye the next time I do."

She missed me, but they were picking plaster out of the gumballs for the next three weeks. "You see, Mrs. Levkes, what they are today?" There was a bone sticking out of my mother's arm, and Shifra was uncoiling like a cobra. "Tormenting a crippled widow like that?" The beheyme and his beret could both drop dead; three of me and green stamps didn't touch dead Khavele's spit.

"Enough already." My mother hurt too much to shout.

Shifra shrugged her shoulders. "Aza eydele, you're so refined. You're sure he's really yours?"

My mother aimed a hunk of cast at her head. "Stick it up your hole," I yelled in Polish. "And get out of here or you'll be shitting through your lipstick." I thought that's what I said, anyway. My mother told me later that what came out was, "Branch your furrow and scat, before your lipstick's in the bathroom." No wonder nobody hit me.

By the time we were finished at the hospital, my mother almost liked me again. She had me sign her new cast--"After

all, I got it on account of you"--and I made one last appeal to her
sense of justice and told the real truth: Dr. Mandelbroit had
seduced an innocent shiksa--the secret of my social work was
long since out--and Miss Dehmel wanted to atone for her sins
by doing Sabina and me a favour. "A goyeh, mama, what else
does she understand?"

My mother felt bad for everyone. Sabina deserved better for
a father, Miss Dehmel made a terrible mistake--"Nu, it happens,
and not only to shiksas, nebekh"--and if I could help her to get
on with her life, doesn't a just man consider his donkey? "I
want you should have fun, Yoinele, but don't forget there's a
God in the world. Promise me on the soul of your father"--I
couldn't dance a step unless they had an all-boys conga-line.
My mother hugged me with her working arm and started to cry.
"And take off that beret. You look like a Frenchman."

The morning of the prom I limped my way to school with
a gopher hole on my lips and a dish-rag under my sock, a
legitimate excuse to keep me from dancing. "But you're still
comin, aren't you, Jelly?" The beatsters in my class were a little
bit worried.

"I don't know, man." I tugged at my beret. "The Dr. and
Mrs. split for Kansas, you know"--this was actually true; there
was a psychiatric convention going on, and Mrs. Mandelbroit
wouldn't let Benoit out of her sight--"And this gimp thing--I
could do with a little, uh, laying around. If you know what I
mean."

"Yeah, but there's gonna be beer in the parking lot."

I rolled my eyes.

"No, for real this time." I didn't know there'd been a last
time. "Ramsay's brother already bought it..."

"...And Ramsay's got coolers for his trunk, man. We'll
make you an ice-pack for the sprain. Strictly medicinal, like."
We started laughing like we'd discovered fermentation.

"If it's gonna be cold," I'd never tasted beer in my life,
"Well, all right." I let them convince me, but only if Cameron
McManus picked me and Sabina up in his Buick. "Serves you
right for diggin Stan Kenton."

I kept my promise but forgot my lie, and fell flat on my ass
trying to limbo. Sabina and I held hands in the corner, we got
our picture taken and split a beer in Ramsay's back seat. Sabina

danced a few times, once with Mr. Sherbowits, and Miss
Dehmel was groovin high--I never would have pegged her for
the bunny-hop type--until Colleen Semple, who'd shown up
stag, or whatever you call it for a girl, went mad with jealousy;
she tried to trip Darius Fong and ended up on her knees in the
middle of the dance floor, bawling about her secret crush and
banging her veiny fists into the great plain of her middy. "I'm
blonde, too, you know!" Darius had come with Zsa Zsa from
the Catholic school--nobody but him knew her real name, but
she was blonder than butter and had a shirt full of grace. "You
let her suck your father's egg rolls, Darius?"

Miss Dehmel smelled racial incident and bolted from
Sherbo's arms in the middle of *Purple People Eater*. She grabbed
the microphone, the band kept playing, and the auditorium
started to rock to the rhythmic chant of Colleen's last name:
"Sem-Ple, Sem-Ple." Down on the floor, Sherbowits was
knocking the shoe out of Zsa Zsa's hand, and Darius was
making faces at me and Sabina. He knew that my sprain was
a fake; it had been his idea to ask for the ride. "Hey, Levkes,"
he shouted--Miss Dehmel had quieted the band and was
weeping over the P.A. about Albert Schweitzer and peaceful
coexistence, gunpowder and paper, Marco Polo and spaghetti-
-"Levkes, get over here and suck my egg roll, you limping little
Hebe." Everybody heard him, but only Miss Dehmel looked
hurt. "Egg-Roll, Egg-Roll." It sounded even better than
Semple. Miss Dehmel looked like she'd been hit with a pie; she
stamped her foot and just stood there on the stage, the spotlight
right on her scar, while everybody started to conga to "Suck my
little egg roll." She hadn't been this far away from Sherbowits
since she made him dance with Sabina, and she was more alone
than ever now. As soon as he got Colleen outside, Miss Dehmel
ran after him to help calm the poor girl down.

I was having the time of my life just sitting around. I'd never
seen Sabina in a gown before, and she told me she was wearing
garters. When her ankles started davening in their heels--
Semple wasn't the only one who fell down that night--we knew
it was time to go back to her place. "Nu?" I asked, as we came
up to the doors. They were brand new, all glass. Sabina looked
away from her image and nodded; I'd lent her my shul-key after
class, and she'd never been to the mikve before. "Emes?" I

started gagging so hard, my reflection turned red; we stopped so I could get my breath, Sabina took both my hands and made me tell her how much I loved her, while I coughed all over her face. "And there won't ever be anybody else?" I shook my head and kept coughing. Sabina kissed my forehead and clapped me on the back, my spasms subsided and I walked towards the doors, bright-eyed and hopeful and limping by choice, my love on my arm and a three-pack of condoms in my left front pocket.

GLOSSARY

Alte--old
Amerike goniff--an expression of dismay or incredulity, literally,
    America thief

Baalebuste--housewife
Beheyme--beast, moron, jerk
Bes medresh--house of study
Borukh-a-shem--Blessed be God
Bris--circumcision ceremony
Bubbeh--grandmother

Cholent--baked dish eaten on the Sabbath

Daven--to pray
Dekh--of course

Ekh mir--what a, some
Emes--truth, truly
Erev--eve of
Eysev--Esau

Fir Kashes--the four questions asked at the beginning of the
    Passover seder
Fleysheke--pertaining to meat
Frum--pious, religious

Gantse nakht--whole night

Gematria--"Computation of numerical values of the letters of a word, equating two words on the basis of identical numerical values" (U. Weinreich)

Gemore--loosely, the Talmud

Gemore-niggen--chant used in traditional study of Talmud

Goysess--dying person

Halakha--Jewish law

Hartsveytik--heartache

Herst--you hear?

In gantsn--completely

Kaddish--doxology, often recited for the dead

Kaleh--bride, engaged girl

Khaleh--braided egg bread; TAKE KHALEH--removal of a piece of dough to be burnt, a women's mitsve

Khalileh--God forbid

Khamehs--lowlifes, boors

Khap--to grasp, understand, "catch it"

Khevra kaddisha--burial society

Kheyder--Jewish religious school

Khnyok--sanctimonious religious fanatic

Khreyn--horseradish

Khork--obvious from context

Kiddish--sanctification, a snack or meal served after synagogue services; also, blessing over wine on Sabbath and holidays

Kishkes--guts, intestines

Klipeh--shrew, evil spirit

Kupl--yarmulke

Kvell--swell, usually with pride and pleasure

Kvetch--to complain

Mama-loshn--mother's tongue, Yiddish

Maspid--to eulogize

Mamzer--bastard

Matse--matzoh, unleaved bread

Meshiekh--messiah

Meshiekhs tsaytn--Messiah's times, the messianic age
Mikve--ritual bath
Mileh--circumcision (the thing itself)
Minkhe--afternoon service
Mitsve--commandment, good deed
Moyel--circumciser
Musaf--additional service on Sabbath and holidays
Narishkaytn--foolishnesses

Nebekh--an expression of pity, cf. nebbish

Oymer--sheaf, counted for seven weeks between Pesakh and
  Shavues
Oys--out, no more

Payes--sidelocks
Pesakh--Passover
Pipik--navel
Pogromtchick--pogromist
Poyel--prevail, get one's way

Rakhmones/Rakhmunes--pity
Rebbetsin--rabbi's wife

Seyfer toyre--Torah scroll
Shabbes--sabbath
Shabbesdik--fit for or pertaining to shabbes
Shadkhn--marriage broker
Shakhris--morning service
Shavues--Pentecost
Shaygets--gentile boy, or more generally, a goy
Shikker--drunk
Shkutsim--plural of shaygets
Shmutz--dirt, filth
Shokl--to rock, shake
Sholem Aleikhem--Sabbath hymn sung on returning home from
  the synagogue
Shoymer shabbes--sabbath observant
Shoyn--already
Shtikl Toyre--a bit of Torah

Shtrayml--round fur hat worn by hasidim
Shulkhan Arukh--a Jewish legal code
Smikhe--rabbinic ordination
Standing shminesre--praying the Eighteen Benedictions, the
     central prayer of all services
Sukke--a tabernacle or little hut for the holiday of the same
     name

Takeh--indeed
Taleisim--plural of tallis
Tallis--prayer shawl
Tefillin--phylacteries
Treyf, Treyfene--unkosher, unclean, profane
Tsaddik--righteous man, just man, saint
Tsekokht and tsemisht--hot, bothered and confused
Tsitse--a single ritual fringe
Tsitsis--ritual fringes, or the entire garment to which they're
     attached
Tsuris--troubles
Tukhes--buttocks, ass

Vi heyst--what's he/she/it called?
Vus far a--what kind of a
Yeshiva rebbe--yeshiva teacher
Yiddishkayt--literally, Jewishness; Jewish culture
Yingele--diminutive of yingl, boy
Yoizele--a pejorative name for Jesus
Yortsayt--anniversary of a death

Zayde--grandfather